52 Reflections
on Faith
for Busy Preachers
and Teachers

D1440043

Text copyright © Stephen W. Need 2014
The author asserts the moral right
to be identified as the author of this work

Published by
The Bible Reading Fellowship
15 The Chambers, Vineyard
Abingdon OX14 3FE
United Kingdom
Tel: +44 (0)1865 319700
Email: enquiries@brf.org.uk
Website: www.brf.org.uk
BRF is a Registered Charity

ISBN 978 1 84101 743 3

First published 2014
10 9 8 7 6 5 4 3 2 1 0
All rights reserved

Acknowledgments
Unless otherwise stated, scripture quotations are taken from the New Revised Standard
Version of the Bible, Anglicised Edition, copyright © 1989, 1995 by the Division of Christian
Education of the National Council of the Churches of Christ in the USA, and are used by
permission. All rights reserved.

Scripture quotations taken from the Revised Standard Version of the Bible, copyright © 1946,
1952, 1971 by the Division of Christian Education of the National Council of the Churches of
Christ in the USA, are used by permission. All rights reserved.

Cover background photo: Istockphoto/Thinkstock

Every effort has been made to trace and contact copyright owners for material used in this
resource. We apologise for any inadvertent omissions or errors, and would ask those concerned
to contact us so that full acknowledgment can be made in the future.

A catalogue record for this book is available from the British Library

Printed and bound by CPI Group (UK) Ltd, Croydon CR0 4YY

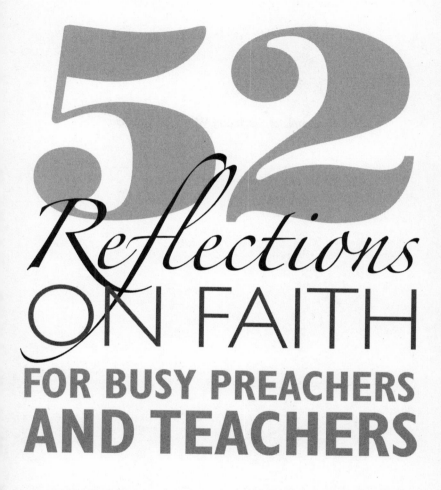

52
Reflections
ON FAITH
FOR BUSY PREACHERS
AND TEACHERS

STEPHEN W. NEED

For the people of Stock and West Hanningfield

Contents

Foreword 8

Introduction: from Sinai summits to the Emmaus road......10

Part 1: Sinai

Advent and Christmas

1 Advent: the coming of God 15

2 Christmas: Mr Scrooge 20

3 Epiphany: the fourth wise man................................24

Lent and Easter

4 Ash Wednesday: depending on God...........................28

5 Passion Sunday: responding to God............................32

6 Palm Sunday: little donkey 37

7 Maundy Thursday: washing the feet 42

8 Good Friday: access to God................................47

9 Easter Day: transforming lives................................51

10 Ascension Day: presence, not absence 56

Pentecost and Trinity

11 Pentecost: a fire deep inside................................61

12 Trinity Sunday: the circle of life................................66

Saints

13 John the Baptist: pointing to Jesus 70

14 Peter: a perfect disciple? 75

15 Paul: enthusiast for faith 79

16 St George's Day: slaying your dragons 84

17 Mary, mother of Jesus: pointing to God 89

18 All Saints Day: humility and service 94

Festivals

19 The Annunciation: fearing God 98

20 Mothering Sunday: the motherhood of God 103

21 Corpus Christi: sanctifying matter 107

22 Transfiguration: shining with God's love 112

23 Remembrance: hoping against hope 117

24 Harvest: saying 'thank you' 122

25 Christ the King: overcoming suffering 126

Part 2: Emmaus

God

1 God and the world: separate or together? 133

2 Seeing God: a way of life 138

3 The big picture: God and evil 142

4 Faith and doubt: seeking understanding 146

5 Treasure: where your heart is 151

6 Repentance: saying you're sorry 155

7 Becoming real: loved into life 159

Jesus

8 Jesus Christ today: knowing, naming and
   following him 163

9 Jesus the teacher: words and deeds 168

10 Jesus and healing: the new creation 173

11 Jesus and the poor: God in suffering 177

12 Jesus the good shepherd: door of the sheep 182

13 Wisdom: Christ himself 187

14 Justification by faith: computer studies 192

15 Light: standing in the river 196

16 Lineage: the Christian family tree 200

Belief and practice

17 Baptism: a new beginning 204

18 The body of Christ: respecting difference 209

19 Humility: the compassionate life 213

20 Loving your enemies: Israelis and Palestinians ... 218

21 Prayer: listening to God 223

22 Icons: looking through a window 227

23 Glorious food: the Eucharist 232

24 Fasting: training the soul 236

25 The ten commandments: doing what you like 240

26 Growth and renewal: good soil 245

27 Emmaus: the eyes of faith 250

Afterword 254

Notes 256

Index of Bible study passages 258

Foreword

This is such a *refreshing* book! With a rich variety of starting points, it offers both preachers and teachers fresh ways into the seasons of the Christian year. Perhaps freshness, especially in sermons, is that which most effectively kindles within the listener new thought on God's ways with humanity. We are fed simply by seeing the gospel from a different direction.

Stephen brings his varied and scholarly background into every reflection, yet he does so always carrying his learning lightly. His wealth of experience, both living in the Holy Land and leading study tours throughout the Levant and notably in those places where Jesus walked the earth, offers a unique take on each of the themes of the different seasons. Both the earliest Christian world and the still more ancient world of Judaism make their mark here.

All this is painted on to a broader canvas. The kaleidoscopic variety of music, visual arts and literature capture one's imagination from the first moments of each reflection. From Ebenezer Scrooge to Stripe the Caterpillar, from Gerard Manley Hopkins to the Rublev icon, from Oberammergau to Billy Elliot and Elton John—and so much more—Stephen promises every time a new insight for those of us called to speak anywhere and everywhere. There is an enormous treasury of resources here to stimulate the teacher or preacher, or simply for any reader to be nourished in the gospel.

The secret behind all this is, of course, Stephen's own humanity, and his reflection upon that through a lifetime of

New Testament and Patristic study. So we encounter both Old and New Testaments focused through the lens of constructive critical scholarship and enriched by the freshness of Stephen's imagination. The brief notes of books for further reading offer the engaged reader modest and realistic ways of following up the patterns of thought that Stephen has pursued. I hope this book will nourish, amuse, surprise and stimulate you as you turn each page, as it has done for me.

Bishop Stephen Platten

Introduction:
from Sinai summits
to the Emmaus road

I hope you will enjoy this collection of 'bite size' reflections on Christian faith. Most of the pieces here have grown out of sermons and addresses I've given or out of Bible studies I've led over a number of years. Some started life in the Holy Land with groups I worked with there. Others began as sermons in the parishes in Essex where I'm now Priest-in-Charge. All are offered here in the hope that a wide variety of readers will enjoy and benefit from them.

Each reflection is intended to provide a short, sharp moment of insight into Christian faith and life. Some draw on biblical texts, some on theological or practical aspects of Christianity. The book is divided into two parts: 'Sinai' and 'Emmaus'. The first part has several sections following the Sundays and other days of the Church's year, including some saints' days and festivals. The second part has three sections: 'God', 'Jesus' and 'Belief and practice'. Overall, the 52 reflections enable a journey through the Christian year and through the Christian life of faith.

Each piece is intended to inform and challenge as well as stimulate and feed the reader, with each giving a particular 'take' on the subject concerned. The reflections are not intended to be, in any way, definitive, either separately or together, but I hope they will provide a new angle on belief or a new insight into faith. The pieces on Christmas, Good Friday, Easter and Pentecost, for example, are not intended to be the last word about how those feasts or events should be understood. Nor are the pieces on God, Jesus, and belief and practice intended to 'say everything'. They are intended to open doors on new possibilities, make connections with different aspects of life, and invite you to consider a fresh approach or understanding to some important parts of Christian life and belief.

Many of these reflections focus on a well-known piece of art or music, a popular song, story or book. Others simply use a provocative idea to set the wheels of the mind turning (and, I hope, of the heart and soul as well). Connections are made between aspects of Christianity and today's life and culture, showing how religious sensitivities and beliefs continue to permeate our lives in different forms. The first piece begins on Mount Sinai, marking the coming of God and the beginning of faith. The last one invites you along the Emmaus Road, marking Jesus' continuous call to a new stage in the journey of discipleship.

The book should be useful to busy preachers, teachers and group leaders, especially when preparing sermons or addresses. It would be good for individual use in private study or meditation but can equally well be used by a number of people studying together—for example, in a church Advent or Lent group. It can be 'dipped into' or followed in order. Groups could create their own short courses by choosing a selection of the pieces for a particular season. Passages for Bible study, questions for discussion and books for further reading are provided at the end of each piece to assist further exploration.

My prayer is that you will find these reflections on Christian faith inspiring and refreshing.

Part One
Sinai

Advent and Christmas

1

Advent: the coming of God

If you stand at the top of Mount Sinai in Egypt in the very early morning on almost any day of the week during the warmer months of the year, you'll probably find yourself in the company of hundreds of pilgrims who have made their way up the 'God-trodden' mountain in search of a divine encounter. The lunar landscape and the dramatic sunrise are part of the final moment in their long journey through the desert in search of God. 'Mount Sinai', or the 'Mountain of Moses' as it's sometimes called, has been marked by Christians since at least the sixth century as the place where God made himself known to Moses when he established the covenant with ancient Israel. The mountain still exudes a striking sense of the 'numinous' or the mystical. It's one of those 'thin' places where the presence of God seems tangible. That's why it's also known as the 'mountain of God'.

In the book of Exodus, Mount Sinai is a special place of revelation and encounter with God. It has a certain mystery about it. Moses prays to God, 'Show me your glory', and God replies, 'You cannot see my face; for no one shall see me and live.' 'You shall see my back,' he adds, 'but my face shall not be seen' (Exodus 33:18, 20, 23). The ancient Israelite experience of God includes their ordeal in Egypt (Exodus 1—12), the exodus and wanderings in the wilderness (chs. 13—18), the establishment of the covenant (chs. 19—24) and the giving of the ten commandments or Decalogue (Exodus 20:1–17; Deuteronomy 5:6–21) at the mountain. Finally, of course, they arrive in the land (Joshua 3—4) and their quest for God continues throughout their history. The ancient Israelite quest for God parallels the human search and longing for God in sacred places and sacred spaces in every age. Modern pilgrims to Sinai and other holy places stand in a long line of human questers for God.

Yet we must never forget that God seeks human beings before they seek him. At the foot of Mount Sinai, St Catherine's Monastery contains the Chapel of the Burning Bush. From the fourth century, Christians have marked that place in memory of the encounter of Moses with God in Exodus 3. As Moses looked after the flock of his father-in-law Jethro in the desert, 'the angel of the Lord appeared to him in a flame of fire out of a bush; he looked, and the bush was blazing, yet it was not consumed' (3:2). In this story, God calls to Moses from the bush. God seeks Moses before Moses seeks God. The bush isn't destroyed but reveals the fire of God burning in creation. The story of the burning bush was taken up by the early Christians in writings and icons as a paradigm of the revelation of God in creation. They knew that it is through creation that God goes on a journey towards human beings long before they start seeking him, speaking to people and drawing them to himself.

In the 19th century, the Jesuit priest-poet Gerard Manley Hopkins (1844–89) also knew of God's powerful presence in creation. Hopkins had a vivid sense of the sacramental nature of creation and experienced God's presence in the physical world in an almost tangible way. His poem 'God's grandeur' reflects this:

> *The world is charged with the grandeur of God.*
> *It will flame out, like shining from shook foil;*
> *It gathers to a greatness, like the ooze of oil*
> *Crushed.*

In spite of the smear that man leaves upon creation, Hopkins continues, 'nature is never spent'. He adds, 'There lives the dearest freshness deep down things.'[1] That 'dearest freshness' continues to spring forth in creation, revealing God to us. Hopkins is aware of the way God's life seeps through the material creation, drawing us to himself. In this sense, creation operates as one of the main vehicles of God's coming to us.

Pilgrims at the top of Mount Sinai, the story of the burning bush and the powerful insights of Gerard Manley Hopkins together remind us of the truth known by the early Christians— that although we frequently think of ourselves as searching for God, God himself searches for us first. As Westerners today, we often imagine ourselves going out in search of the divine. We go on pilgrimages to holy places; we attend retreats for meditation and contemplation and perhaps visit church more often. We might even fast or do good works to help bring God into our lives. We imagine we're the ones who are in control of finding God.

We forget, though, that it is God the creator who first goes out from himself in creating us and making us in his image. It is God the creator who calls to us from creation itself and makes us aware of his presence. It is God, in his generosity and grace, who makes himself known to us and invites us to be with him. Wherever we are, God calls to us from within creation, from within our relationships, from within our communities and from within the sacraments of our church. Our quest for him is enabled by him and is, in fact, our response to his own prior call. Whether we're at the top of Mount Sinai or simply at home getting on with everyday life, God seeks us and calls us to himself long before we go in search of him.

The Church's season of Advent is all about God's coming, about his movement towards us as well as our searching for him. Pilgrims and seekers and all who search intently for God, in whatever way, should remember that it is God who takes the initiative: he calls us and we respond. In Advent we wait, listen and wonder in anticipation for God's coming once again into our lives, and we prepare our response of thanksgiving, faith and love.

Bible study passages

- Exodus 3:1–15
- Exodus 33:17–23
- Mark 13:24–37

Questions for discussion

- Where do you mostly experience God's presence?
- In what ways and at what times have you specifically 'searched' for God?

- Identify a time when you have felt God searching for you.
- How far do you agree with Hopkins that 'the world is charged with the grandeur of God'?
- What are your experiences of God's absence?

Further reading

Gerard Manley Hopkins, *Poems and Prose* (ed. W.H. Gardner) (Penguin, 1985)

Michael Sadgrove, *Lost Sons: God's long search for humanity* (SPCK, 2012)

2

Christmas: Mr Scrooge

One of my favourite Christmas characters is Mr Ebenezer Scrooge in Charles Dickens' short novel *A Christmas Carol*. Scrooge is a legendary figure, known to everyone as the all-time miser. He's remembered largely as a misery during the season of the year when goodwill is expected from everyone—but there's more to Scrooge than is usually appreciated. By the end of the story, he has made a dramatic turnaround in his life, reminding us that we can all change if we want to. Christmas should give us a positive attitude towards the world and the people around us, not leave us buried in our own selfishness.

Scrooge's story begins on Christmas Eve, when he's counting his earnings and being generally miserable about the upcoming feast. Focused on his own selfish interests, he considers Christmas a lot of 'humbug'. He's even loath to give Bob Cratchit, one of his employees, a paid day off on Christmas Day. But the same evening, as Scrooge sits at home wallowing in his selfishness, the ghost of his former partner, Mr Marley, appears to him, warning him that if he doesn't change his ways he'll end up where Marley is, in personal torment.

Three other ghosts appear that evening, taking Scrooge on a series of imaginary trips that confront him with what will happen to him if he doesn't change. The Ghost of Christmas Past shows Scrooge things from his earlier life that make him uncomfortable, the Ghost of Christmas Present confronts him with his life as it is now, and the Ghost of Christmas Yet to Come shows him what will happen in the future.

The various ghostly appearances have a transforming effect on Scrooge and he wakes up on Christmas Day a changed man, exuding love and compassion for his fellow human beings. He even sends the Cratchit family a turkey for their Christmas dinner. The spirit of Christmas has changed Scrooge from a miserly, self-centred individualist to an outgoing, friendly figure, loved by everyone. Far from being a miser, he ends up as the epitome of the Christmas message. The great feast has worked its wonder on him and imprinted on him its message of love and compassion. The whole story has a serious message for us all at Christmas: it is possible to move out of our tiny worlds of selfishness into the God-given world of compassion and love for everyone.

There's another aspect to Scrooge's story that parallels perfectly the message of Christmas. The Gospel reading for Christmas Day is John 1:1–14, including the famous verse that sums up the Christmas message: 'And the Word became flesh and lived among us.' The message is that God has taken flesh and come to earth in lowly and humble form.

The Gospel reading tells us that in eternity there is both God and the Word. The Word is God's rational side, God's orderly governing aspect through which he created the universe. In John's Gospel, the Greek word *Logos* lies behind the word 'Word'. John tells us that the Word 'was with God' and also 'was God' (v. 1). Next we learn that God's Word is his instrument of creation—the tool, as it were, with which he creates all things: 'All things came into being through him, and without him not one thing came into being' (v. 3). It's a powerful claim: nothing that exists is separate from God, and God is responsible for everything that exists. In creating the world, God becomes thoroughly involved with the world.

This is the basis of the claim in verse 14 that 'the Word became flesh', for in the incarnation God comes again in Jesus. The birth of Jesus in Bethlehem is not God's first coming to creation. He is already in creation from the beginning. So, in the birth of Jesus there's an intensification of God's coming: 'grace upon grace' (v. 16). In creating the world and in coming in Jesus, God shows that he loves the world and that the creation is good. We first learn this from the account of creation in the book of Genesis (for example 1:4, 10). Now, in John's Gospel, it is reaffirmed: when the Word becomes flesh, God announces that creation, including flesh, is good. This is the heart of the Christmas message—that God loves the world, that he takes on flesh and affirms the world.

People often think these days that if they're to be truly 'Christian' they must reject the things of the world. Today's Christians in particular often separate religion and spirituality from the material aspects of creation. We may (without even realising it) operate from within a dualistic worldview, separating God and spiritual matters from the rest of the world. But Dickens' Mr Scrooge actually gets it right: he moves out from himself and embraces the world. It's possible for all of us, when we accept the message of the gospel at Christmas, to remain trapped in our own selfishness, simply translating our existing habits into a religious mode: we become even more pious or simply do more religious things. Mr Scrooge, however, travels in the right direction, away from his selfishness toward the needs of others. He is a fine example for us all.

The message of Christmas calls us to reorient our lives,

to journey away from our selfish pursuits and towards involvement in the needs of others. Indeed, God himself moves away from himself in creating the world and in coming to it again in the birth of Jesus. At Christmas we hear once again the message that God loves the world, affirms the world and takes the world on as he takes on flesh and is made known in a human life. At Christmas God affirms the world, acknowledging again its goodness and its value. Just as, in the end, Mr Scrooge worked out the meaning of Christmas and got the message right, so can we.

Bible study passages

- Genesis 1:1–13
- Matthew 19:16–22
- John 1:1–18

Questions for discussion

- Why did Mr. Scrooge change his ways?
- What is the main message of Christmas?
- What do you understand by 'the Word became flesh'?
- What effect should Christmas have on our lives?
- If creation is 'good', what do we do with the 'bad' things?

Further reading

Charles Dickens, *A Christmas Carol*, with an Introduction by Anthony Horowitz (Puffin, 2008)

Tom Wright, *John for Everyone: Part 1. Chapters 1—10* (SPCK, 2002)

3

Epiphany:
the fourth wise man

The feast of the Epiphany on 6 January is a celebration of the 'manifestation' or 'shining' of Christ to the Gentiles. In the Eastern churches it's also Christmas Day. The baptism of Christ is another closely associated feast. In the Western imagination, Epiphany marks the coming of the wise men to the manger as recounted in Matthew 2:1–12. Churches often put their figures of the three kings into their crib scenes on this day. Everyone knows the story of the three wise men, but how many know the story of the fourth wise man? His story isn't in the Bible but it teaches us a great deal about the gospel message of the revelation of Christ and about the responsibilities Christians have towards others.

The story of the other wise man begins in the east, in Persia, in the city of Ecbatana. The fourth wise man is called Artaban, and he is a magician or astrologer like the other three. Zoroastrian by faith, he meets with scholars who are reading the signs of the times and watching the stars. They discern that an important king will soon be born, one who will be a light to the nations. The birth will take place as the planets

Jupiter and Saturn pass. When the time comes, Artaban sets off to meet the other three wise men and make the journey with them to Bethlehem of Judea, where the king will be born.

Artaban decides to take three jewels with him on his journey: a blue sapphire, a red ruby and a white pearl. He hides them in his cloak and sets off to Babylon on horseback to meet up with the other wise men. On the road in Babylon, he comes across a body. Thinking it dead, he gets down from his horse to move it. However, he finds the man still alive and in need of water, food and care. He drags him to a nearby tree, thinking that he will be late for his meeting with the other three wise men and will fail to arrive in Bethlehem on time. Could a single act of help ruin his quest? Yes, it could!

After helping the man, he continues into the city and does indeed find that the other three wise men have gone on ahead of him. They've left a message telling him to cross the desert and follow them, but Artaban's horse is exhausted and he realises he'll need a camel to make the journey. He sells the sapphire, buys a camel and heads off into the desert towards Damascus, Mount Hermon, Galilee and Judea.

When he arrives in Bethlehem, Artaban finds that not only have the three other wise men gone to Egypt but so has the newborn king, fleeing the soldiers of Herod the Great who has announced that he will kill all male children under two years old. In Bethlehem, Artaban meets a young woman with a baby son. She takes him into her house, telling him she's afraid the soldiers will come and kill her child. When a soldier arrives, Artaban gives him his second jewel, the ruby, telling him there's no child there. The soldier leaves without checking the house. Artaban then sets off for Egypt, committed to his quest for the newborn king. When he arrives, he encounters all manner of sickness, poverty, plague and famine, and sees imprisonment and death. Still, he is determined to find the king.

After 33 years of searching, Artaban still hasn't had any success, but he decides to go to Jerusalem to continue his quest. When he arrives, he hears that Jesus of Nazareth is to be crucified there that day. Artaban thinks he's reached the end of his journey. As he makes his way through the Jerusalem crowds, a young slave girl in need of food falls at his feet, begging him to help her. He hesitates, thinking once again that he will miss his moment and fail to find the one he seeks. He offers the girl his final jewel, the pearl, to help her.

Just then, the earthquake that struck at the time of Jesus' crucifixion shakes the city. Buildings tremble and crumble. Tiles fall from roofs and the fourth wise man is hit on the head. As he falls to the ground, bleeding, he hears a voice saying, 'Truly I tell you, just as you did it to one of the least of these who are members of my family, you did it to me' (Matthew 25:40). At that moment he realises he has found the king, that he has in fact been encountering him in the dying, the needy and the sick throughout the years of searching.

The Story of the Other Wise Man was written by Henry Van Dyke (1852–1933), an American professor of English Literature at Princeton. His story has an important message for Christians today. We all have religious and spiritual goals we wish to reach. We all want to make the journey, spiritually or even physically, to Bethlehem or somewhere else. Often we're so eager to get to our own religious destination that we have no time for those we encounter along the road of life. Like the fourth wise man, we don't want to be interrupted or delayed.

The truth is, however, that it is in the interruptions, the opportunities to help others, the sick, the dying and the needy that we will find Christ. It is there in the faces and lives of those around us that we will encounter him. It is in helping the people in need that our real religious goal will be reached. It is in those opportunities that the true light of God will shine for us.

This is the message of Van Dyke's wonderful story of the fourth wise man; it is the gospel message of Matthew 25:31–46, and it is also the meaning of the feast of the Epiphany.

Bible study passages

- Isaiah 60:1–6
- Matthew 2:1–12
- Matthew 25:31–46
- Luke 10:25–37

Questions for discussion

- What is the meaning of the story of the three wise men?
- When have you felt merely distracted by someone and thus lost the opportunity to help them?
- What are your spiritual quests or goals?
- To what extent do you think Matthew 25:31–46 is the heart of Christianity?
- What projects for helping people does your church or community have?

Further reading

Henry van Dyke, *The Story of the Other Wise Man* (Bridge-Logos, 2000)
Tom Wright, *Matthew for Everyone: Part 2. Chapters 16—28* (SPCK, 2002)

Lent and Easter

4

Ash Wednesday: depending on God

Ash Wednesday is the first day of Lent, the period of 40 days before Easter. Lent is a season of fasting and repentance in preparation for the joyous celebration of the resurrection of Jesus on Easter Day. The 40-day period comes from Jesus' 40 days in the wilderness, being tempted by the devil (Mark 1:12–13). Ash Wednesday gets its name from the use of ash as a symbol during the Eucharist on the day itself. Those present are invited to have their foreheads marked with a cross of ash, reminding them of their mortality and their dependence on God. Traditionally, the ash is made when palm crosses from the previous year's Palm Sunday are burnt.

As each person is marked with a cross in ash, the following words are said: 'Remember that you are dust and you will return to dust.' Like bread, wine and water used in the church's services, ash is a very powerful physical symbol, and the words spoken over each person remind them that they too have come from dust and will become dust again when they die. They are reminiscent of the words in the funeral service: 'ashes to ashes, dust to dust'.

Ashes have probably been used as a religious symbol since life began, or, rather, since fire was discovered. As soon as fire was used to burn things, there would have been ash, and it seems that ash carried with it some of the mystery of fire. Fire and ash were both thought of as sacred and were used by different peoples around the world to symbolise a variety of things. For example, we know that ash was used by various tribes in Africa, by people in South America and by Europeans from very early times.

Ancient Israel used ash regularly as a symbol of humility, repentance, purity, fasting, mourning and grief, as is clear in the Old Testament. In the book of Genesis, Abraham refers to himself as 'dust and ashes', meaning that he is insignificant before God: 'Let me take it upon myself to speak to the Lord, I who am but dust and ashes' (18:27). The ashes of the red heifer were seen as purifying (Numbers 19:9–10). In the book of Esther, Mordecai puts on sackcloth and ashes (4:1) and in the apocryphal book 'The Rest of Esther', Esther herself puts ashes on her head as a symbol of humility and repentance (14:2). Perhaps most famously of all, Job, afflicted with sores, sits on a pile of ashes scraping his wounds (Job 2:8). When it looks to the prophet Jeremiah as though Jerusalem will fall to the enemy, he encourages people to 'roll in ashes' (Jeremiah 6:26), and in the book of Daniel, the prophet seeks an answer from God 'by prayer and supplication with fasting and sackcloth and ashes' (9:3). In the book of Jonah, when the people of Nineveh turn to God, a fast is proclaimed. Then the king takes off his robes and sits in ashes (3:6).

In some societies, animal and human ashes were rubbed on to the human body in order to stimulate circulation or in the belief that this action would stave off disease and bring health. Human ashes have been considered sacred. They have been buried or scattered and sometimes thrown into rivers or the sea. Some families have put the ashes of their loved ones into urns in temples or shrines, in the belief that the presence of the deceased person would continue. The ashes have sometimes been thought to yield special physical or moral virtues when visited. In all these ways, ashes are seen as sacred, powerful and life-giving.

There is very little mention of ashes in the New Testament but the meaning is the same as that in the Old Testament. In the Gospels of Mathew and Luke, Jesus condemns the towns Chorazin and Bethsaida in Galilee for their lack of faith and says that if the mighty works done in them had been done in Tyre and Sidon, those places would have repented in sackcloth and ashes (Matthew 11:21; Luke 10:13). Here, ashes are clearly associated with repentance.

The Ash Wednesday 'ashing' ceremony has become standard practice for marking the beginning of Lent in many churches around the world. When this is done, the symbol operates at a number of different levels. The ash invites humility, repentance, fasting and purification. A sense of mourning and grief might also play a part in repentance for sin, but the most significant level of the symbolism is that it reminds us of our mortality and dependence on God. Through the ash, we Christians are confronted with our individual and corporate need of God. We are dependent upon God for the gift of life itself, for our bodies, souls and spirits and for the continuing blessings we receive.

Receiving the cross on our foreheads on Ash Wednesday

invites us into repentance and a changed life along the way of the cross with Christ to Easter. As the words spoken over each person indicate, we are made from dust and will return to dust. We are mortal and dependent upon God, the giver of life. We are created by God and return to God. The ash of Ash Wednesday reminds us of our createdness, our creatureliness and our mortality. It invites us to recommit ourselves to following God in Christ at the beginning of Lent, throughout the year and for the rest of our lives.

Bible study passages

- Job 2:1–10
- Joel 2:1–2, 12–17
- Matthew 4:1–11

Questions for discussion

- What is your experience of ash being used in church on Ash Wednesday?
- To what extent is ash a useful symbol?
- Identify other symbols used in church. What are their meanings?
- Think of the many ways in which we are dependent upon God. Which are the most important?
- In what ways does a sense of mortality affect your faith?

Further reading

Ruth Burrows, *Before the Living God* (Continuum, 2008)
Christopher Irvine (ed.), *The Use of Symbols in Worship* (SPCK, 2007)

5

Passion Sunday:
responding to God

In the summer of 2010, the famous Passion Play at Oberammergau in Bavaria, Germany, was performed for yet another
very successful season. The residents of the village have presented their play of Christ's suffering, death and resurrection
every ten years since 1634 to increasing numbers of people
from around the world. The story of how the play came into
existence is fascinating. In the early 17th century, the bubonic
plague struck the area and the villagers prayed to God that
they would be delivered. They were, and in response they
vowed to perform a passion play as a thanksgiving every ten
years thereafter, for ever. With few exceptions they have kept
their vow and thousands of pilgrims now travel to see the
performance, which is repeated daily over several months. A
combination of dramatic stage presentations and wonderful
music lasting several hours, the play is well worth making the
journey to watch.

The drama itself is a moving spiritual experience but the
story of its origins carries an important message: the people
of Oberammergau experienced God coming to them in their

hour of need and responded by committing themselves to his service. In this way, the villagers, then and now, challenge us all to respond to God in our own ways, wherever and whenever we can. God takes the initiative and we respond.

During Passiontide it's a good idea to read one of the Gospel accounts of Jesus' last days. The Gospel of John is more dramatic than the others, containing layer upon layer of symbolism, paradox, irony and double meaning. In the second century, Clement of Alexandria in Egypt referred to it as the 'spiritual Gospel' and commentators ever since have acknowledged its theological depth.

Throughout this Gospel there are numerous occasions when Jesus triggers responses from people—for example, Nicodemus (3:1–15), the Samaritan woman (4:1–42), the man born blind (9:1–41), Mary Magdalene (20:11–18) and Thomas (20:24–29). In John's 'passion play' the responses are particularly noticeable. The opening scene is set in the garden, where Judas appears with a band of soldiers (18:1–8). Jesus takes the initiative and speaks to Judas first. 'For whom are you looking?' he asks the soldiers, and they reply, 'Jesus of Nazareth.' Jesus replies, 'I am he' (vv. 4–5). In using these words from Exodus 3:14, he is alluding to Moses' encounter with God at the burning bush. When Moses asks God who he shall say has sent him to the people of Israel, God says to tell them, 'I AM has sent me to you.' 'I am' is therefore the divine name, which Jesus uses more than once in this Gospel—for example, saying, 'I am the light of the world' (8:12) and 'I am the resurrection and the life' (11:25). Now, at the beginning of John's passion play, Jesus uses the name on its own: 'I am he'. The scene is an encounter with God to which there is a dramatic response: the soldiers fall back, to the ground. This sets the tone for the whole passion narrative in which Jesus takes the initiative and triggers various responses from those around him.

Earlier in the Gospel, in chapter 13, instead of recounting the last supper as we know it from Matthew, Mark and Luke, John has Jesus washing his disciples' feet, an act of humility in which he takes dramatic initiative and the disciples respond. Peter objects (v. 8) and Judas emerges as the one who is to betray Jesus (vv. 21–30). Later, in the passion narrative itself, Peter denies Jesus three times (18:15–27). Pilate's response is perhaps the most dramatic of all. His famous question 'What is truth?' (v. 38) is riddled with ambiguity.

On other occasions, too, John's passion narrative teaches us something important about God's initiative and people's response. In 19:31 and 42 we learn that it was 'the day of Preparation' for the Passover when Jesus died. The author has changed the chronology of events here so that Jesus dies at the same time as the Passover lambs die, not the day after the Passover meal, as in the other Gospels. In other words, Jesus himself is a Passover lamb sacrificed for the feast. Indeed, he has been the 'Lamb of God' from the beginning of this Gospel (1:29, 36). Then, in the crucifixion scene itself, Jesus' words to his mother and the beloved disciple, 'Here is your son' and 'Here is your mother' (19:26–27), result in the beloved disciple's taking Jesus' mother into his home. Throughout this Gospel, then, we see different responses to God's initiative through Jesus.

As the people of Oberammergau felt God's presence with them when the plague was averted and responded to him by committing themselves to perform the play every ten years, and as Jesus takes the initiative in John's 'passion play' and people respond in their various ways, so we also, in our own time, must find our ways of responding to God. There are many ways in which we might do this: in worship we might fall to our knees in the presence of God; in daily life we might serve someone in need, care for a sick person or help someone in danger. We might contribute to the life of our church or community with the many gifts we each individually have. Like Jesus' disciples, too, in making our responses to God we might question and protest, deny and betray as we struggle to find our way, but our response will be crucial in deciding what sort of disciples we really are.

The divine drama invites us to play a part in it. The divine life gathers around us and we enter in. God's initiative awakens us and triggers our response. Passiontide asks us to look seriously at what God has done for us and what we might do for God.

Bible study passages

- Genesis 12:1–9
- John 18:1–11
- John 18:15–27

Questions for discussion

- What are your reactions to the story of the Oberammergau Passion Play?
- In what ways have you responded to God's initiative?
- How far should we take God's call literally?
- What different responses to Jesus are there in John's Gospel?
- What can be learnt from thinking of John 18—19 as a drama?

Further reading

Raymond Goodburn, *A Pilgrim's Guide to Oberammergau and its Passion Play* (Pilgrim Book Services, 2008)
Jim Wallis, *Faith Works: Lessons on spirituality and social action* (Random House, 2000)

6

Palm Sunday: little donkey

Sometime in the late 1990s the local municipality of Jerusalem denied all donkeys access to the walled Old City. The decision was made primarily on health grounds but it changed the landscape of Jerusalem immediately. Somehow the donkey was a feature of the desert and of the Bible; its presence contributed to the 'Bible Lands' ethos of Jerusalem valued by so many Christian pilgrims. Didn't Jesus ride into Jerusalem on a donkey on the first Palm Sunday? Yes, and with great significance and symbolism. His kingdom was a kingdom of humility and peace, a kingdom of patience and suffering, a kingdom of service and loyalty to God. All these characteristics, especially humility, are symbolised by the donkey. On that first Palm Sunday Jesus didn't ride into Jerusalem on a horse, the symbol of worldly authority and power. He rode in on a donkey or ass, the symbol of humility and lowliness.

In their book on the last week of Jesus' life (called *The Last Week*), the well-known New Testament scholars Marcus Borg and John Dominic Crossan point out an important contrast which brings Jesus' Palm Sunday ride into Jerusalem on a donkey into real focus. They remind us that there might well have been two processions entering Jerusalem that day—one with Jesus entering the city on a donkey, and the other with the Roman Prefect Pontius Pilate riding in on horseback with all the paraphernalia of military power. Pilate would have made his way to Jerusalem from his residence in Caesarea Maritima on the coast, something he often did at Jewish festivals with a view to keeping the peace.

This time, though, Jesus of Nazareth arrived too, announcing his kingdom of humility and peace. He had preached the kingdom of God in Galilee and was now to act it out symbolically. The contrast is striking. There could be no doubt about Jesus' intentions. Indeed, his whole life had been in contrast with the ruling powers of his day. He had been born in Bethlehem near one of the palaces of Herod the Great, whose kingdom, like Pilate's later on, was built on worldly power. The two kingdoms were diametrically opposed—one earthly and based on war, the other 'of God' and based on humility. Palm Sunday invites us to consider the difference.

All four Gospels tell of Jesus' entry into Jerusalem (Mark 11:1–11; Matthew 21:1–11; Luke 19:28–40; John 12:12–19). The setting is the Mount of Olives, itself a symbol in biblical literature for the coming of God. In Judaism, it is from the east that the Messiah will come and, in later Christian thinking, Jesus will return there, so the Mount of Olives is the location of the coming of God and is an obvious setting for Jesus' Palm Sunday ride. Mark names the place as somewhere near Bethany and Bethphage at the Mount of Olives. Jesus sends two disciples ahead to get an ass. When they bring it, they put their garments over it and he sits on it and rides into the city. Others lay their garments on the road and wave palm branches, shouting, 'Hosanna! Blessed is the one who comes in the name of the Lord!' (Mark 11:9).

King David also went to the Mount of Olives and was

given asses there (2 Samuel 15—16). He was on his way out of Jerusalem, in flight from his son Absalom, who was trying to take his father's kingdom. David had his weaknesses but was seen as an ideal king. The Gospel writers present Jesus as a new David, but one whose kingdom is different from his predecessor's. In Matthew's version of the entry into Jerusalem, Jesus is the 'son of David' fulfilling the prophecy of Zechariah: 'Tell the daughter of Zion, Look, your king is coming to you, humble and mounted on a donkey' (Matthew 21:5; Zechariah 9:9).

The event of Jesus riding into Jerusalem is often known as 'the triumphal entry' but it must have been anything but triumphant in the worldly sense. It wouldn't have attracted much attention at the side of Pilate's military show of power. Jesus' procession must have been a minor affair in terms of numbers and probably went unnoticed by many in Jerusalem that day. Pilate's procession is more likely to have provoked responses, but the symbolism of Jesus' donkey ride, like the symbolic acts of many of Israel's prophets of old, struck a deep chord with those who were with Jesus. Here was a 'king' who was different. Here was a 'son of David' who was different. Here was a leader who trod a different path and rode a different animal.

Jesus' preaching and teaching in Galilee had spoken of his kingdom; his healings and miracles had demonstrated it, and now he was to take his message to its logical conclusion. Jesus' 'triumphal' entry into Jerusalem was marked by humility and service of the God whose presence he embodied throughout his life. It was symbolised in the donkey ride into Jerusalem at the beginning of Holy Week.

It's a shame that donkeys have disappeared from the Old City of Jerusalem. They remind pilgrims not only of Jesus' ride into the city but of his entire purpose and of the kingdom he came to establish. G.K. Chesterton's poem 'The Donkey' tells how, in spite of the animal's image as the 'tattered outlaw of the earth', the beast itself knew how special the moment was when 'there was a shout about my ears, And palms before my feet'.[2] The donkey played an important role in Jesus' preaching of the kingdom of God. Legend has it that the cross marked in the fur on the donkey's back comes from Jesus sitting on it, and some churches in England include a real donkey in their Palm Sunday processions. There's something to be said for this as a powerful symbol of what Jesus stood for.

Donkey or no donkey, Palm Sunday gives us an opportunity to think of the significance of Jesus' ride into Jerusalem, of the kingdom he preached and embodied, and of the nature of our own discipleship along the road to the cross.

Bible study passages

- 2 Samuel 15:30—16:4
- Zechariah 9:9–17
- Matthew 21:1–11

Questions for discussion

- What is your understanding of the symbolism of the donkey?
- In what way was Jesus' entry into Jerusalem 'triumphal'?
- What do you understand by the description of Jesus as 'son of David'?
- How fair is it to say Jesus was a 'pacifist'?
- What is the message of Palm Sunday for Christians today?

Further reading

Marcus J. Borg and John Dominic Crossan, *The Last Week: What the Gospels teach about Jesus's final days in Jerusalem* (SPCK, 2008)

Walter Wink, *Jesus and Non-Violence: A third way* (Fortress, 2003)

7

Maundy Thursday: washing the feet

Maundy Thursday is the first of the three holy days leading up to Easter. Christians usually think of it as the day when the Eucharist was instituted. Jesus ate a meal with his disciples in Jerusalem the night before he died, thereby inaugurating the Christian practice of gathering together to eat a meal in his name. The setting of Jesus' last meal was the Jewish feast of the Passover in about AD30. The annual Passover celebrates the liberation of the ancient Israelites from slavery in Egypt. It commemorates the crossing of the Red Sea, the establishment of the covenant between God and his people, the giving of the law and the entry of the people into the promised land. Passover looks back to the events of the formation of the people of Israel but also forward to God's continuing care for his people in the future.

According to the Gospels of Matthew, Mark and Luke, the meal Jesus ate with his disciples on the night before he died was actually a Passover meal (Matthew 26:17; Mark 14:12; Luke 22:7). However, in the fourth Gospel this is clearly not the case. John changes the chronology of events, and the meal with the disciples takes place the night before the Passover meal (13:1; compare 19:14). As a result, Jesus dies with the Passover lambs in preparation for the Passover meal, thus fitting in nicely with John's theme of Jesus as the Lamb of God (1:29, 36).

John tells us something else about the meal Jesus had with his disciples. It's something that gave Maundy Thursday its name, and it concerns the 'new commandment'—in Latin, the *mandatum novum*. This is the day when Jesus gave his new 'mandate' or 'Maundy' to his disciples: the mandate is the commandment to love one another. Jesus says, 'I give you a new commandment, that you love one another. Just as I have loved you, you also should love one another' (John 13:34). There's a well-known modern hymn based on these words.

John's Gospel brings out the theme of the 'new commandment' very clearly. When we read this account of the last supper, it's very noticeable that there is no bread and wine mentioned. Jesus doesn't take bread and wine or say 'This is my body' or 'This is my blood'. Indeed, there is no meal as such, as there is in the other Gospels. The meal is clearly not the most important thing for John. He includes teaching elsewhere on Jesus the bread of life (ch. 6) and Jesus the true vine (ch. 15) but it's clear that the washing of the feet is the most important thing here in chapter 13. For the first readers or hearers of this Gospel, especially if they knew the other Gospels, there would have been something of a surprise at the message here: you won't understand the meal unless you understand the foot-washing.

In the account in John's Gospel, it's during supper that Jesus lays aside his outer garments and girds himself with a towel, the towel of washing and service. At meals in those days, the washing of guests' feet was carried out by a servant, not the host of the meal: Jesus takes the place of the servant. Luke also emphasises this aspect in his last supper scene, where Jesus says, 'For who is greater, the one who is at the table or the one who serves? Is it not the one at the table? But I am among you as one who serves' (22:27). So also in the washing of the feet scene in John's Gospel, Jesus is a servant. He washes his disciples' feet and then takes up his garments again. Some commentators have seen the laying aside of garments and the taking of them again as symbolic of Jesus laying aside his divinity and taking it again, something that Paul writes about in Philippians: '... Christ Jesus, who, though he was in the form of God, did not regard equality with God as something to be exploited, but emptied himself, taking the form of a slave, being born in human likeness. And being found in human form, he humbled himself and became obedient to the point of death— even death on a cross' (Philippians 2:5–8).

In the supper scene in John's Gospel, Jesus humbles himself in the form of a servant by washing his disciples' feet, and then the mandate is given. But what is new about it? The Jewish law had emphasised love of God and neighbour (Deuteronomy 6:4–5; Leviticus 19:18). The newness of Jesus' command, surely, is that there is an active side to it. Jesus effectively says, 'Love your neighbours in this way: wash their feet.' It is through Jesus' humility as shown in this scene that we begin to see God in him.

In the 16th century, the Italian painter Jacopo Tintoretto did six paintings of Jesus washing his disciples' feet, for different churches in Venice. One of them ended up in the National Gallery in London. It depicts Jesus on the floor; the disciples are gathered in the darkness on one side of the painting while he is in the centre, in the light, which is intended to portray his divinity. Tintoretto brings it out well: it is in Jesus' humility that we start to see his divinity.

Maundy Thursday is certainly about the institution of the Eucharist. It also has Passover themes of freedom and liberation. But the message of the foot-washing is crucial. The message of Maundy Thursday and of the washing of the feet is surely that we shall never be among Jesus' disciples unless we are humble. Paul says that we are baptised into Christ's death (Romans 6:3–4), which makes the point even more strongly. As Christians we are invited into a humble life, and only through this shall we understand the Eucharist properly. Indeed, is this not the identifying characteristic of Christians, that we have love for one another in the style of the mandate given to us by Jesus on Maundy Thursday?

Bible study passages

- Deuteronomy 6:1–9
- Leviticus 19:13–18
- Luke 22:24–27
- John 13:2–20

Questions for discussion

- What is the message of Jesus' actions in John 13:2–20?
- What experiences of humility have you had?
- How important is humility for Christians today?
- In what ways could Christians serve people in your community?
- What limits are there to humility and serving people?

Further reading

Alan G. Padgett, *As Christ Submits to the Church: A biblical understanding of leadership and mutual submission* (Baker, 2011)

Tom Wright, *John for Everyone: Part 2. Chapters 11—21* (SPCK, 2002)

8

Good Friday: access to God

The 16th-century German artist Matthias Grünewald painted the crucifixion of Christ for his famous Isenheim Altarpiece. It is one of the most shocking, realistic images of the crucifixion you are likely to see. Christ himself is twisted on the cross, his head down. The angular thorns on his crown draw blood from his head. His hands are open wide, his fingers extended in pain. The blood pours from his pierced side, down to his feet. Thorns also pierce his flesh all the way up and down his body. His face is ghastly, exuding an image of exhaustion and death. Adding to the image of tragedy and loss are further sores permeating his entire body. The whole scene is an image of misery and desperation.

The painting was commissioned by the monastery of St Anthony in Isenheim, near Colmar in Alsace, France. The special ministry of the monks there was to provide hospital care for sufferers of skin disease and plague. Seeing the body of Jesus in Grünewald's painting as they prayed, patients were strengthened in the knowledge that Jesus knew their sufferings.

Today, the Isenheim Altarpiece is a stark reminder to Christians of the realities of death by crucifixion. Barely any of our church crucifixes portray the real agony of this form of death. Good Friday is the day to contemplate the realities of Jesus' crucifixion and its meaning, and the Isenheim Altarpiece and the Gospel narratives help us to do this.

First, it is important to know that in the Judea of Jesus' day, crucifixion was a common and horrific form of capital punishment. Judea was occupied by the Romans and it was they who made crucifixion their supreme form of punishment for criminals. During the time when Jesus lived, thousands went to their deaths on crosses of various shapes and sizes. Someone might be put to death for betraying the government, for violence or for leading a rebellion. It was a bloody, cruel and slow way of dying. It could take considerable time for a person to die of crucifixion, and in the end the exhaustion would give way to asphyxiation or heart attack. For those who looked on, crucifixion was a form of deterrent designed to put off would-be criminals. It could also provide a form of entertainment for the local populace as they mocked and taunted the victim.

Second, one of the comments made by the first three Gospel writers, Matthew, Mark and Luke, is that at the time of Jesus' death the curtain of the Jerusalem temple was torn in two from top to bottom (Matthew 27:51; Mark 15:38; Luke 23:45). This comment tells us something very important about how they saw the significance of the vicious and cruel death that Jesus underwent.

The Jerusalem temple was thought of as the very dwelling-place of God himself and was laid out as a series of graded courts in a rising hierarchy of significance. The various courts were named after those who were forbidden from passing any further. The largest, outer court of the temple was the Court of the Gentiles, beyond which Gentiles could not pass. Then came the Court of the Women, the Court of the Israelites, the Court of the Priests and the temple court. Finally, there was the dwelling-place of God himself, the inner sanctum or Holy of Holies. This was the most sacred place of all and no one was allowed to enter it except the high priest, and he only once a year on the Day of Atonement or Yom Kippur.

Between the court of the temple and the Holy of Holies, a curtain hung. Jewish tradition says that it was a hand's breadth thick. Some Jewish sources say there were two curtains but, in any case, there was a clear separation between the ultimate dwelling-place of God and the other areas. Even more important was the separation between God and humanity that the curtain symbolised. There was, as it were, a great barrier fixed between God and the human race. The Gospel writers' comment that, at the time of Jesus' death, the temple curtain was torn in two tells us that, in Jesus' death, humanity is brought into the very presence of God. The separation between God and humanity is taken away. The writer of the letter to the Hebrews not only sees Jesus as the one who has entered the curtain; he sees Jesus' flesh as the curtain itself (Hebrews 10:20).

On Good Friday, when we look at the cross of Jesus and ask its meaning for us today, two things are important. First, it's important to realise the extent of the suffering Jesus underwent in his crucifixion, which the Isenheim Altarpiece illustrates so vividly. Jesus' suffering was enormous and epitomises all our suffering. Second, we need to understand the meaning of the Gospel writers' comment that the curtain of the temple was torn in two, opening up the place where God dwells and allowing human access to God.

We can say that, combining these two things, Jesus' death shows us something important about what God is like: he knows suffering and pain, and can identify with our own weaknesses. It is striking, too, that it is often in the times of our greatest pain and loss that we come to know God. In the cruel suffering and death of Jesus on the cross, a door is opened into the very life of God himself: a curtain is torn in two. Good Friday is 'good' because its message is one of pain and death leading to resurrection and new life. In the horrific death of Jesus, depicted for us by Grünewald and other artists, the curtain of the temple is torn in two from top to bottom and the way to God is opened up for all who have faith.

Bible study passages

- Matthew 27:45–54
- Mark 15:33–39
- Luke 23:44–49
- John 19:28–30

Questions for discussion

- What was Jesus death actually like?
- What images of the crucifixion are you familiar with?
- What is the message of Good Friday today?
- Is it enough to say that Jesus' death provides 'access to God'? Give reasons.
- In what senses is Good Friday 'good'?

Further reading

Sheila Cassidy, *Good Friday People* (DLT, 1991)
Henry Wansbrough, *The Passion and Death of Jesus* (DLT, 2003)

9

Easter Day:
transforming lives

Once upon a time, a small caterpillar popped out of its egg and found itself sitting on a leaf. It had striped fur and was called Stripe. As Stripe made his way slowly along the branch of the tree and down the trunk, he looked into the distance and saw an amazing sight—a huge pillar of caterpillars climbing on top of each other, trying to get to the top of the pillar. It was a caterpillar pillar! Stripe made his way over to the caterpillar pillar and started to climb up. Other caterpillars told him they didn't know what was at the top but they knew they had to get up there anyway.

As Stripe climbed, he found others pushing each other and treading each other down. Suddenly, as he was about to put a foot on to the head of another caterpillar, he looked into her lovely yellow eyes and thought, 'She looks nice. I can't tread on her.' They started talking and Stripe soon discovered that her name was Yellow. As no one seemed to know what was at the top of the caterpillar pillar, Stripe and Yellow decided they would make their way down to the bottom again.

At the bottom, Stripe and Yellow rested a while. Yellow was

content to stay there but Stripe still wanted to know what was at the top of the pillar. He set off again, without Yellow, to have another go at reaching the top. Meanwhile, something very strange happened to Yellow: an unusual covering wrapped itself around her and she was gradually transformed into the most beautiful yellow butterfly. Up on the caterpillar pillar, Stripe climbed for ages. Other caterpillars were still treading each other down, trying to get to the top.

Suddenly, as Stripe was nearly at the top, he looked out and saw the most beautiful yellow butterfly flying towards him. He looked into her eyes and thought, 'I know those eyes. It can't be… It can't be… It's Yellow.' How beautiful she looked! Stripe then made his way down to the bottom of the pillar again and something strange started to happen to him too. An unusual covering started to surround him and he also was transformed into a beautiful butterfly.

That's my version of the story of Stripe and Yellow (*Hope for the Flowers* by Trina Paulus) and how they were transformed from their caterpillar bodies to their beautiful butterfly bodies. It's a powerful story for Easter Day, speaking to us of transformation from one sort of body to another. No wonder Christians have used the butterfly as a symbol of the resurrection of Jesus.

Easter Day is the celebration of the resurrection. The message of Christians is that Christ is risen. Today we hear in church services the great resurrection stories of the Gospels, stories of the empty tomb, the appearances of Jesus and the disciples' realisation that Jesus was alive again. It was a shocking and exciting experience for the disciples and they reacted to it in different ways. The women at the empty tomb in Mark's Gospel were too afraid to say anything (16:8). In Matthew's Gospel they went and told everyone (28:7–8). In the appearances on the road to Emmaus in Luke 24:13–35 and at the tomb in John 20:11–18, Cleopas, the disciple with him, and Mary Magdalene didn't even recognise Jesus. The resurrection is a mysterious transforming event that shocks and excites.

It is Paul who takes us to the heart of the matter, in 1 Corinthians 15. This chapter is a vision of the resurrection and its meaning. Paul himself underwent a dramatic, life-changing experience of Jesus on the road to Damascus (Acts 9:1–9). He knew from personal experience the radical transformation he had undergone as he moved from being a persecutor of Christians to being a follower of the risen Christ. In 1 Corinthians 15:5–7, Paul writes of the appearances of the risen Christ to various people, and of the significance of the resurrection to the Corinthians, whose minds were muddled on the subject. Paul encourages them to understand their own resurrection in relation to the resurrection of Christ. He connects the whole subject with Adam and outlines the resurrection of Christ as crucial for the whole human race: Adam was the 'first man'; Christ is the 'second man' (1 Corinthians 15:45–49).

In the second half of the chapter, Paul draws attention to a simple fact: there are different types of bodies in the world. There are human bodies and animal bodies, birds and fish, heavenly bodies and earthly bodies. There is the sun and the moon and there are different sorts of stars. 'Not all flesh is alike,' says Paul (v. 39). Then comes the crucial element: there is a physical body and there is a spiritual body (v. 44). The spiritual body is the resurrection body, but it is more than just spiritual in the usual sense of the word. It's still a 'body' but a different sort of body—a perfected body.

For Paul, the resurrection of Jesus is about the corruptible body putting on incorruption, about the perishable becoming imperishable, and about what is dying coming to life through death. Paul's message is that the resurrection of Jesus brings all creation through its perishable state into the fullness that God has planned for it from the beginning. What is 'sown in weakness', says Paul, alluding to the cycle of the natural world, 'is raised in power' (v. 43).

The wonderful story of the transformation of Stripe and Yellow from caterpillars to butterflies parallels the Christian message of the resurrection. It tells us that change can take place in our lives, that we can be transformed into something new and can mutate into something beautiful. The message of the resurrection of Jesus is that God gives new life, transforms us into something different and draws all creation up with him in the resurrection of Jesus. No wonder the butterfly became a symbol of Jesus' resurrection.

Bible study passages

- Mark 16:1–8
- John 20:11–18
- 1 Corinthians 15:35–50

Questions for discussion

- What are your reactions to the story about Stripe and Yellow?
- What is your understanding of the resurrection of Jesus?
- Is it necessary to believe in the physical resurrection of Jesus in order to be Christian?
- In what ways have you experienced transformation in your life?
- In what ways are Christians 'risen with Christ'?

Further reading

Paula Gooder, *The Risen Existence: The spirit of Easter* (The Canterbury Press, 2009)

Trina Paulus, *Hope for the Flowers* (Paulist Press, 1972)

10

Ascension Day: presence, not absence

Ascension Day is one of the most important days in the Church's calendar. It has been celebrated since the fourth century and has played a significant part in the life and culture of many Christian countries. It forms a fundamental part of the New Testament message about Jesus, although the actual story is only found twice, once in Luke 24:50–53 and once in Acts 1:9–11. Like other events in the life of Jesus, the ascension has been painted by numerous artists who have tried to bring out its meaning. There are many icons, frescoes and mosaics depicting the ascension, and a famous painting (1636) by Rembrandt in an art museum in Munich, Germany.

What are we to make of the ascension of Jesus and what is its message for us today? We often think that it is about the departure of Jesus from the world at the end of his earthly ministry, and it's easy to see why this is the case. We are told by Luke in the Acts of the Apostles that 40 days after Jesus' resurrection, he went out to the Mount of Olives and a cloud took him from his disciples' sight (Acts 1:9). It looks as if Jesus disappeared, but this concentration on departure is a complete misunderstanding of the meaning of the ascension. It isn't really about Jesus going away or about his absence. It's about the completion of his coming and about his continuing presence in the world.

There are several 'ascensions' in the Bible and in later Jewish and Christian literature. In Genesis, Enoch is taken up into God's life (5:24) and, most famously, Elijah ascends into heaven in a chariot of fire (2 Kings 2:11). In later Jewish literature, other figures, such as Abraham, Moses, Raphael and Isaac, ascend into heaven. In each case, the meaning of the story is that the person concerned is considered to have a particularly close relationship with God. The person enters the presence of God more deeply when they pass from this world to the other, so ascension stories are about God's closeness to his people, not his distance from them.

In the New Testament, the emphasis is the same. Although Jesus' ascension is found only in Luke–Acts, the language of ascension is everywhere—for example, in John's Gospel, where there is frequent mention of Jesus descending and ascending (see 6:38, 62). Paul writes in Philippians 2:9 of Jesus being 'highly exalted', and the author of Hebrews refers to Jesus as the 'great high priest who has passed through the heavens' (4:14). Always the emphasis is on God's presence rather than his absence.

The meaning of Jesus' ascension can be found specifically in some of the symbols in the story itself. First, the location: the event takes place on the Mount of Olives, across the Kidron Valley, east of the Temple Mount in Jerusalem. This mountain, like others in the biblical narratives, is a key place in God's coming to earth. In Judaism, Christianity and Islam over the centuries, the Mount of Olives has been considered as a prime location for the coming of God. In Judaism, the Messiah will come from the east to Jerusalem, and 'from the east' means to the Temple Mount across the Mount of Olives. In Christianity, the notion of Jesus' return, arising partly out of the ascension narratives (see Acts 1:11), has also been associated with the Mount of Olives. So also in Islam, Jesus' return at the end of time will be across the Mount of Olives.

This special mountain, therefore, is a place of revelation and expectation. It's a holy place and forms part of the sacred geography of the area. It is significant that Luke puts Jesus' ascension on the Mount of Olives: the event points to the revelation or coming of God in Jesus. It's not about Jesus' departure and absence but about his continuing presence with his disciples.

Another element in Luke's account of the ascension in Acts is the cloud that takes Jesus from the disciples' sight. In the Bible, the cloud symbolises the very presence of God (the later Hebrew word used for it is *shekinah*), and the cloud is mentioned in this symbolic way in several places: the dwelling of God is in the tent in the desert (Exodus 33:9–11); God is present on Mount Sinai when the covenant is established (Exodus 24:15–18) and in the Jerusalem temple when the ark is brought there (1 Kings 8:10). The cloud symbol is also used to indicate God's presence in a great deal of later Jewish and Christian mysticism.

One of the most well-known Christian mystical writings using the cloud symbol is the anonymous 14th-century book *The Cloud of Unknowing*.[3] The cloud symbolises the deep and mysterious presence of the unknowable divine essence, which the mystic enters in prayer. So when Jesus enters the cloud at his ascension, he is taken into the very life of God. The event is reminiscent of the coming of 'one like a son of man' (RSV) on clouds in Daniel 7:13 and of the clouds in Revelation 1:7.

Jesus' ascension is about the entire cycle of God's involvement with the world, bringing it to partial completion but moving the process on to its next stage.

The story of Jesus' ascension has an important message for Christians today. It isn't about Jesus disappearing from view, his departure or absence. Rather, it is a sign of God's affirmation of everything Jesus has done in his life, death and resurrection, as portrayed in the Gospels. It confirms God's coming to us and his continuing presence with us in Christ, and the New Testament certainly envisages that we followers of Jesus can ascend with him when the time comes (John 14:2–3; 1 Thessalonians 4:17) if we follow his example. By following in Jesus' way, we shall know God's continuing presence with us.

Bible study passages

- 2 Kings 2:1–14
- Luke 24:50–53
- Acts 1:9–11

Questions for discussion

- What paintings or icons of the ascension of Jesus have you seen?
- What is your understanding of the ascension?
- What does the ascension of Jesus add to his resurrection?
- In what ways are the ascensions of Elijah and Jesus the same as or different from each other?
- How important do you think the ascension of Jesus should be for Christians?

Further reading

Douglas Farrow, *Ascension Theology* (T&T Clark, 2011)
Tom Wright, *Acts for Everyone: Part 1. Chapters 1—12* (SPCK, 2008)

Pentecost and Trinity

11

Pentecost: a fire deep inside

One of the most moving songs in the popular musical *Billy Elliot* by Lee Hall and Elton John is 'Electricity', sung by Billy at his audition at the Royal Ballet School in London. Set during the 1984 miners' strike in England, the musical is about a young boy in the north of the country who wants to be a dancer. Everything is stacked against him but he has real talent and finally gets to go to London for an audition. On the day, he has a disappointing interview and feels that he'll never succeed, but, as he leaves the room, one of the interviewers asks him what it feels like when he's dancing. He replies by singing 'Electricity', saying that he feels a deep change inside him, like fire burning. Words are not enough to describe the transforming experience he goes through but he feels released and alive. It's confusing and disorienting but also inspirational, opening him up in an amazing way. Billy whirls across the stage, showing what a superb dancer he is—and, of course, he gets accepted.

Billy's song reminds us of the tremendous power of the Holy Spirit moving in our lives today. It's difficult to describe; it's often confusing and disorienting but it changes us deeply. Sometimes we don't know what's happening to us but it makes us feel free. Pentecost is the celebration of the coming of the Holy Spirit into our lives and into our church. It celebrates the tremendous transformative power of the Holy Spirit and looks for its continuing presence in our midst. 'Pentecost' means '50 days' and the festival comes 50 days after Easter. Originally the Jewish feast of Pentecost was a spring harvest festival. It came 50 days after Passover, which was connected with Mount Sinai. The first Christians took Passover and made it Easter; they took Pentecost and made it the coming of the Holy Spirit. In Acts 2:1–13 the Holy Spirit comes on the first disciples in Jerusalem 50 days after the resurrection, falling on them like great tongues of fire, transforming their lives and their entire sense of God.

In the Old Testament, the Spirit of God moves first upon the waters of creation when God makes the world (Genesis 1:2). It is then present in the leaders of Israel, such as the judges (Judges 3:10; 6:34) and kings. It rests upon Saul and David (1 Samuel 10:6, 10; 16:13) and upon prophets such as Hosea, Micah and Ezekiel (Hosea 9:7; Micah 3:8; Ezekiel 2:2). Later it's associated with the end of time, when it will be poured out upon everyone (Joel 2:28). For the Jews of the Old Testament, the Spirit was a dynamic, life-giving force, the force of God himself coming upon his people.

In the New Testament, Jesus is conceived by the Holy Spirit (Luke 1:35), is baptised by the Spirit (Mark 1:9–11) and sends his disciples out to baptise in the name of the Holy Spirit

(Matthew 28:19). His entire ministry is characterised by the Holy Spirit. In Luke 4:14–19 he stands up in the synagogue in Nazareth and reads a key text from Isaiah 61:1–2: 'The Spirit of the Lord is upon me...'. He is led by the Spirit out into the wilderness to face the devil in the temptations (Mark 1:12–13) and he is in regular conflict with evil spirits (Mark 1:21–28; 5:1–20). The Holy Spirit comes upon the whole community in Acts 2:1–13, indicating a global dimension to its work. People of many nations and languages are present as the Spirit is poured out and the curse of the tower of Babel is taken away (compare Genesis 11:1–9). Also in Acts, leaders such as Peter and Paul are filled with the Holy Spirit (4:8; 9:17). In John's Gospel, Jesus sends 'another Advocate' (or 'paraclete', 'comforter' or 'helper') to be with the disciples after he has gone (John 14:15–17). This is the Holy Spirit.

The experience of the Holy Spirit has changed the lives of thousands of people down the centuries. In early Christian theology, it was thought of as one of God's special ways of relating to the world. Alongside God the Father and Jesus, the Spirit gave people an experience of God active in their midst. Increasingly the Spirit was seen as the strengthener and sanctifier, operating together with God the Father (the creator) and God the Son (the redeemer). The Holy Spirit was the one who continued to bring the presence of God to his people, playing a significant part in the theology of the Trinity. It was at the Council of Constantinople in 381 that the divinity of the Spirit was affirmed. Traditionally (see 1 Corinthians 12:8–10), the 'gifts of the Spirit' have included wisdom, knowledge, healing, miracles, prophecy, discernment, tongues (and their interpretation) and love, and in Galatians 5:22–23 Paul speaks of love, joy, peace, patience, kindness, generosity, faithfulness, gentleness and self-control as 'the fruit of the Spirit'.

At Pentecost we celebrate the coming of the Holy Spirit, moving ever fresh and ever new in our lives, inspiring, strengthening and sanctifying us. The Spirit moves in creation to create and recreate, to mould and to shape, enabling us to respond to God's gift of himself to us. The Spirit brings creation to its completion, to what God always intended it to be, completing God's creative and sanctifying acts towards us. Beginning in creation, the Spirit is completed in being continually poured out upon us in the life of the church. We are, then, creatures of the Spirit, who bear the fruit of the Spirit and constantly try to collude with the Spirit's work in God's creative acts among us.

Pentecost is a wonderful celebration of life and creativity, art and music, colour and dance. It is a celebration of the beauty of the universe as the Spirit of God breathes through it. On the feast of Pentecost, like Billy Elliot, we feel a fire burning deep inside us and we know that it is the Spirit of God.

Bible study passages

- Joel 2:28–32
- Acts 2:1–13
- John 16:7–15

Questions for discussion

- What is your experience of the Holy Spirit?
- Do you have to be religious to experience the Holy Spirit? Give reasons.
- Is it true to say that Billy Elliot experienced the Holy Spirit when he danced?

- What do the words 'advocate', 'paraclete', 'comforter' and 'helper' tell us about the Holy Spirit?
- Where do you think the Holy Spirit is working today?

Further reading

Michael Ramsey, *Holy Spirit: A biblical study* (SPCK, 2010)
Tom Wright, *Acts for Everyone: Part 1. Chapters 1—12* (SPCK, 2008)

12

Trinity Sunday:
the circle of life

Probably the most popular icon of the Holy Trinity these days is the one by the Russian iconographer Andrei Rublev, which is displayed in the Tretyakov Gallery in Moscow. Reproduced widely, it has become very well known in recent years outside the Orthodox Church. Andrei Rublev was born in the 14th century and the icon was originally on the iconostasis (the screen that separates the altar from the main part of an Orthodox Church) of a monastery north-east of Moscow. Today the icon is protected by glass in the gallery and is visited by thousands of Christian and other admirers from all over the world.

Rublev's icon shows the three persons of the Holy Trinity—Father, Son and Holy Spirit—sitting around a table. The scene also depicts the Eucharist and is based on the story of the three mysterious visitors to Abraham in Genesis 18. In the background are the oak trees of Mamre (mentioned in the Bible story) and a building. The colours include different shades of green, yellow and blue. The icon exudes a sense of order, peace, beauty and serenity and reflects the eastern understanding of the Holy Trinity as a community of being among the three persons, a circle of life. In recent years, praying with this icon has become widespread as more and more people have become aware of it.

The background in Genesis 18:1–15 is crucial. One day Abraham is sitting at the door of his tent in the desert when he sees three men approaching. He goes out to meet them and he and his wife Sarah offer them water and bread and slaughter a calf in their honour. They sit down to eat together, and then God predicts that Sarah will have a son. Sarah laughs at this because Abraham is 99 years old and she is 90—far too old for childbearing—but Sarah does later bear a son, called Isaac. This story is known as the 'hospitality of Abraham' and illustrates the famed hospitality of the desert. One particular aspect stands out: the three men who appear in the story are mysterious. They are sometimes called men, but in other translations they are 'messengers' or 'angels'. Even though it is three men who appear, it is 'the Lord' who speaks and announces that Sarah will have a child.

The 'hospitality of Abraham' soon became a 'type' of the Holy Trinity in early Christian theology: the three mysterious figures came to symbolise the three persons of the Trinity. In this desert scene, the early Christians saw the threefold nature of God, revealed long before the coming of Jesus. The three figures formed a powerful connection for them between the Old Testament revelation of God and their own experience. It isn't difficult to see how icons of the Trinity based on Genesis 18 could quickly become popular. The theme found its way on to numerous icons and frescoes around the world, but Rublev's version is now by far the best known.

In the icon the three figures sit around a table. At one level they are clearly angels—each has golden wings and a halo on his head, indicating holiness—but Rublev brings out a number of other important elements showing that the icon reflects a particular understanding of God. The three figures look fairly equal but it isn't clear which is which. Many think that God the Father must be at the centre, the Son on the right and the Spirit on the left, but it may be that the Father is on the right of the icon, the Son in the centre and the Spirit on the left.

When you look closely, there is a circular movement between the figures in the icon, starting from the right. The figure on the right looks to his right towards the central figure. Then the figure in the centre looks to the figure on his right—that is, towards the figure on the left of the icon. Then the figure on the left of the icon looks across the table to the figure on the right, completing the circle. In other words, there is visible circular movement, anti-clockwise, starting on the right and moving to the left, indicating a dynamic relationship between the three figures. This movement reflects the eastern understanding of the Trinity: it isn't a hierarchy of persons, one above the other, but a dynamic circle of relationships, each person dwelling in the other. It's a circle of life. The icon shows a God who relates within himself and to those around him in a number of different ways. Whoever looks at the icon is also drawn into the company of the three figures: there's an empty space at the front of the table. On the table itself is a cup or plate with bread, and it is striking that the entire table between the three figures is formed in the shape of a cup. This brings out the eucharistic aspect of sharing in the meal.

Trinity Sunday is a good day to take a look at Andrei Rublev's icon, to meditate upon it and to ask what it is saying to us about the nature of God. The icon has an amazing richness in terms both of art and of theology. There are many layers and it's well worth taking some time to discover them and reflect on them. At the aesthetic level, its form and beauty provide perfect harmony to the onlooker. Its gentle colours attract the eye and soothe the soul. Its serenity and peacefulness make it a useful focus for prayer. Even more important, though, it portrays some fundamental aspects of the Christian understanding of God. For the Christian, God is one who comes in mysterious ways, has different dimensions to him and invites us to be a part of his company. The Christian God is one who invites us to sit at the table of the Eucharist with him and draws us into his presence in an ever-expanding circle of life.

Bible study passages

- Genesis 18:1–15
- Exodus 20:3–6
- Colossians 1:15–20

Questions for discussion

- What icons have you seen and where?
- What are your feelings about praying with icons?
- What are your reactions to a trinitarian reading of Genesis 18?
- 'Icons are much more than just religious art.' What do you understand by this statement?
- Some people see icons as idols. Do you agree? Give reasons.

Further reading

John Baggley, *Doors of Perception: Icons and their spiritual significance* (Mowbray, 1987)
Ann Persson, *The Circle of Love: Praying with Rublev's icon of the Trinity* (BRF, 2010)

Saints

13

John the Baptist: pointing to Jesus

The bones of John the Baptist have been discovered in Bulgaria, or so some newspapers have implied. A number of remains, including a knuckle bone, have been found in a sarcophagus in the grounds of a monastery on an island called Sveti Ivan, off the coast of Bulgaria in the Black Sea. What an amazing story! It's certainly exciting for Christians.

It seems that the bones were found a couple of years ago and have now been carbon dated by an Oxford professor. It turns out that they date to the first century and may well be from the Holy Land. All this is fascinating for historians, archaeologists and Christians alike. Already pilgrims are pouring into Bulgaria to see the relics. Of course, it's clear that even with this level of dating it can't be known for certain that these are the bones of John, but it reminds us that he's an important historical figure who announced the coming of Jesus. What is his message to us today?

John was essentially a pointer, pointing forward to Jesus and the kingdom he preached. It's useful, first of all, to think of what pointers are. They are signs that show the way to something beyond themselves. We often encounter pointers and signs in daily life. For example, when we're driving we need the signs of the Highway Code. They direct us, enable us and point us to the right places. A sign on the motorway might point us to the location we're trying to get to, such as London, Cambridge or Southend. It might tell us what speed to drive (a sign signalling an action we must take). It might say that elderly people or children are crossing, or that rocks are likely to fall in the area and we need to watch out for them. In all these cases, the sign points beyond itself to something far more important.

In the Gospels, John the Baptist points to Jesus. He appears early on in Mark's Gospel, preaching 'a baptism of repentance for the forgiveness of sins' (1:4). He gathers disciples and baptises them in water. He baptises Jesus. He wears a garment of camel's hair with a leather belt, and his diet is locusts and wild honey. He is a desert figure, portrayed in a way reminiscent of the prophet Elijah in the Old Testament, who was fed by the ravens in the desert and heard the silence of God at Mount Horeb (1 Kings 17:1–7; 19:1–18). John, the new Elijah, dominates the opening of Mark's Gospel but he has been arrested by the time Jesus' ministry starts, apparently because he has spoken out against the divorce and remarriage of Herod Antipas. We learn of this event later in the Gospel, when we are also told that some people think Jesus is Elijah (Mark 6:14–29). As Elijah was the one who was to come at the end of time, so John effectively announces the end of time.

At the beginning of Matthew's Gospel, there's a conversation between John and Jesus. John questions whether Jesus ought to be baptising him, but Jesus wants him to do it: 'Let it be so now; for it is proper for us in this way to fulfil all righteousness' (Matthew 3:15). In Luke's Gospel, we're not told that John baptised Jesus, although there is a reference to the event (3:21–22). In John's Gospel, the baptism is recounted at second hand (1:29–34), but we do have the famous 'testimony given by John' (see 1:19–28), in which John is asked whether he is Elijah and whether he is the unknown prophet who is to come. To each question John answers that he is none of these. He says only that he is 'the voice of one crying out in the wilderness, "Make straight the way of the Lord"' (1:23). John is also mentioned in Acts 19:1–7. Through all of these appearances, his main purpose is to point to Jesus. He decreases as Jesus increases (John 3:30).

There is more about John. The first-century Jewish writer Josephus tells us that John was beheaded at Machearus, Herod's fortress east of the Dead Sea. John's beheading certainly captured the Christian imagination in the early centuries and he also appears in later art and iconography, where he is often depicted with two heads, one on his body and the other on a plate. Tradition maintains that he was buried in Samaria, although his head is thought to be in the great Umayyad mosque in Damascus. In the Orthodox tradition, John is known as the *prodromos* or 'forerunner', again emphasising his role as a pointer to Jesus.

John's role as a sign or pointer shows us that we too can point to Jesus and his kingdom. In daily life, wherever we find ourselves, we can point the way to him. This doesn't always have to be in dramatic public ways, as it was with John. It can be in subtle, quiet ways. Our witness at home or at work might be gentle and silent, providing support and help for someone in need. It might be help given to a stranger or advice given to a colleague. It might be avoiding the sort of religiosity that puts non-believers off faith altogether, embracing instead a manner of compassionate listening and affirmation. There may well also be times when a much more strident witness is needed in the face of social injustice, violence or the suffering of an innocent person. Our witness might be through quiet words, silent example, lobbying an MP, writing a letter to a newspaper or speaking at a meeting. It might also be through getting actively involved in a good cause.

We shall probably never know whether the bones recently discovered in Bulgaria are those of John the Baptist or not, but in the end it's John's role as a pointer that really matters. He is an example to us, pointing to Jesus and the kingdom of God. We can do the same—and our witness, like John's, will not be for our own glorification but for God's.

Bible study passages

- Isaiah 40:1–8
- Mark 6:14–29
- John 1:19–28

Questions for discussion

- Why do human beings need special pointers to things?
- How important are relics of the saints?
- What role does John the Baptist play in the Gospels?
- What traditions are there about John the Baptist?
- Consider the different ways in which Christians can point to God and to Jesus.

Further reading

Shimon Gibson, *The Cave of John the Baptist* (Random House, 2004)

W. Barnes Tatum, *John the Baptist and Jesus: A report of the Jesus Seminar* (Polebridge, 1994)

14

Peter: a perfect disciple?

If you walk into St Peter's Basilica in Rome, you'll be standing on a site associated for nearly two thousand years with arguably the most important of Jesus' disciples. Peter is the most frequently mentioned disciple in the Gospels. Originally from the village of Bethsaida near the Sea of Galilee, he started as a simple fisherman but eventually travelled to Rome and was martyred there in the middle of the first century. In the third century, the Church Father Origen said that Peter was crucified in Rome on an 'upside down' cross—that is, a cross opposite in form to Jesus' cross. Peter didn't think himself worthy to be crucified in the same way as Jesus.

Peter's tomb was known in Rome from the second century, and in the fourth century the emperor Constantine the Great built a basilica over it. Constantine's building was renewed at various times over the years and the current church dates largely from the period following the Reformation in the 16th century. In 1939, archaeologists discovered what they thought were the bones of Peter underneath the basilica, although the bones' authenticity is still widely disputed. St Peter's is now part of the Vatican and is reckoned to be one of the largest churches in the world. Two epistles in the New Testament bear Peter's name, and tradition has it that he informed the writer of Mark's Gospel. So who was Peter and what does he teach us about Christian discipleship today?

We know most about Peter from the New Testament Gospels and the Acts of the Apostles. Above all, he's a strikingly realistic character whose changeable personality and weaknesses come over clearly, and yet he became a key member of Jesus' band of disciples and of the later church. Peter was Andrew's brother and they were the first disciples to be called, along with James and John, another pair of brothers (Mark 1:16–20). Peter is also called Simon Peter, Cephas, and Simon son of John. He was married (Mark 1:30) and had a house in Capernaum, a fishing village on the Sea of Galilee, where Jesus made his headquarters.

Peter was one of the 'inner group' of Jesus' disciples, with James and John. The three are mentioned together in the Gospels on a number of occasions: at the transfiguration (Mark 9:2), at the raising of Jairus' daughter (5:37) and in the garden of Gethsemane (14:33). They were joined by Andrew on the Mount of Olives for a private conversation with Jesus about the signs of the end of time (13:3). Peter was the spokesman for the disciples and, on a famous occasion near Caesarea Philippi, when Jesus asked his disciples, 'Who do people say that I am?' it was Peter who replied, 'You are the Messiah' (although Jesus reprimanded him because he didn't really understand what his Messiahship meant: Mark 8:27–33).

In Matthew's Gospel, Peter attempts to walk on water but fails after a few steps. Jesus says, 'You of little faith, why did you doubt?' (14:22–33). Peter's part in the passion narratives also shows some of his weakness. As he is waiting in the courtyard of the high priest, warming himself by the fire, a maid asks him if he is part of Jesus' group. He denies that he even knows

Jesus, and this happens three times. Then there is a cockcrow and the dramatic words, 'The Lord turned and looked at Peter' (Luke 22:61–62). Peter is reminded of his threefold denial of Jesus after the resurrection (John 21:15–19).

Overall, Peter is a committed but oscillating character, capable of saying one thing and doing another, someone who is perhaps unreliable but picks himself up and has another go. He is capable of surprising actions and of getting hold of the wrong end of the stick, but it's in this sense that he's a good example of discipleship in general. Many of us struggle with contradictory elements in our personalities, especially when we want to be committed to something but then find ourselves too weak to put it into practice. This is certainly the subject of Paul's struggle, which he expresses as feelings of personal division. Writing about life under the Jewish Law and under sin, he says:

I do not understand my own actions. For I do not do what I want, but I do the very thing I hate. Now if I do what I do not want, I agree that the law is good. But in fact it is no longer I that do it, but sin that dwells within me. For I know that nothing good dwells within me, that is, in my flesh. I can will what is right, but I cannot do it. For I do not do the good I want, but the evil I do not want is what I do. Now if I do what I do not want, it is no longer I that do it, but sin that dwells within me. (Romans 7:15–20)

Paul puts into words here something of Peter's character, and yet Peter, one of the inner band closest to Jesus, also confesses Jesus as the Christ and, in Matthew 16:13–20, is given the keys of the kingdom. Later, in Christian tradition, he was martyred and became known as the Prince of the Apostles.

It's very striking that someone with as many human weaknesses as Peter became so important among Jesus' disciples.

There's surely a message in this for us all today: Jesus' disciples are not drawn from among those who always keep their word and never make mistakes, nor from among the unerring or sinless. On the contrary, Jesus' disciples, Peter their chief, are from among those who fail constantly but drag themselves up and have another go. Peter is a perfect example of a struggling human being and he can be an encouragement to us all along our own paths of discipleship.

Bible study passages

- Matthew 14:22–33
- John 21:15–19
- Acts 3:1–10

Questions for discussion

- How would you sum up Peter's character?
- Consider some examples of discipleship.
- What is 'faith'?
- In what ways can weakness be a strength?
- How can Christians best live a life of discipleship today?

Further reading

Stephen Cottrell, *Come and See: Learning from the life of Peter* (BRF, 2011)

Michael Perham, *Jesus and Peter: Growing in friendship with God* (SPCK, 2012)

15

Paul: enthusiast for faith

If you get a chance to travel across Turkey or Greece 'in the footsteps of St Paul', you'll learn a great deal about the man who spread Christianity around the Mediterranean world in the early years after Jesus. You'll become aware particularly of Paul's physical stamina and enthusiasm for his faith. There's a great deal to be learnt from Paul, apart from his amazing theological acumen: he was a committed individual, ready to travel significant distances, ready to make his home wherever he found himself, and ready to meet people wherever he found them. He wasn't only a brilliant thinker and evangelist, he was also a pastor who worked on the ground with the various different and often divided groups he met. His enthusiasm is striking, not only in his letters and his way of life; it can also be seen from the terrain he travelled through.

A 'footsteps of St Paul' course could take you more than halfway across modern Turkey and Greece. You might start in Paul's traditional birthplace, Tarsus, and make your way west through a number of important and impressive archaeological sites. You would do best to follow both the Acts of the Apostles and Paul's own letters in trying to find out where Paul went. In

Acts, he travels on three famous 'missionary journeys' across Turkey and Greece (Asia Minor and Macedonia), making his headquarters in Antioch in Syria.

On the first journey (Acts 13—14), Paul travels from Jerusalem up to Antioch and then, with Barnabas, to Cyprus, starting at Salamis and moving on to Paphos and Perge (near modern Antalya) on the south coast of Turkey. He then goes north to Pisidian Antioch, Derbe and Lystra. On the way back he retraces his steps. On his second and third journeys (Acts 15:36—18:22; 18:23—21:16), he travels further afield, going through some of the same places but stretching beyond, to the west coast, to the metropolis at Ephesus and on to Greece through Philippi and Thessalonica and down to Corinth and Athens. He then makes his way back to Jerusalem. Paul's final journey is to Rome (Acts 27—28). It includes his visit to Crete and, of course, the famous shipwreck off Malta (27:27–44). Tradition has it that he was martyred in Rome in about AD65.

Travelling through any of these places today will bring you to amazing archaeological sites and immerse you in the landscape where Paul worked. If you read from Acts or one of Paul's letters, the sense of his physical and geographical location is vivid. Some scholars doubt that the journeys in Acts are accounts of real journeys that Paul made but, in any case, it's clear that he was an enthusiastic traveller. On occasion, in Turkey, a guide stops to show a group a mountain pass that Paul must have travelled through if he had taken that route. He travelled thousands of miles by foot, possibly by horse and camel and also by boat. However you look at it, Paul covered some ground!

Following in the 'footsteps of Paul' will certainly give you a sense of his physical stamina. Reading his letters will also give you a sense of his enthusiasm for his faith. Paul's writings make up about a quarter of the New Testament, and he is the most important person in early Christianity after Jesus. If Jesus is seen as the founder of the new religion, then Paul certainly helped to spread it far and wide by writing letters to various communities.

Of the 27 writings of the New Testament, 13 are attributed to Paul. Those definitely by him are 1 Thessalonians, 1 and 2 Corinthians, Romans, Galatians, Philippians and Philemon. Colossians and Ephesians are disputed. The following are thought by many scholars to be by the hand of later writers, writing in Paul's name: 1 and 2 Timothy and Titus (the Pastorals) and 2 Thessalonians. Letters thought not to be by Paul are said to be 'Deutero-Pauline'. Because they reflect different circumstances, they're thought by some to reflect different authorship as well. If we look at the definitely Pauline letters, the sheer depth and scope of Paul's theology and pastoral care soon hit us. He grapples with practical concerns and tries to deal with disagreements between different groups in the community, as, for example, in Corinth, where there were issues about Christian worship, sexuality and a whole range of other problems.

Throughout Paul's letters and Acts there's a sense that he is a totally committed individual, striding out physically and mentally in the name of spreading the gospel of Jesus Christ wherever it may take him. Paul's enthusiasm shines through at every level. The *Oxford English Dictionary* defines 'enthusiasm' as 'inspiration', 'intensity', even 'possession by a god'. Whether Paul was 'possessed' is debatable but he was certainly passionately committed to the cause—some would say fanatical. He had spent all his energy persecuting Christians until his life-changing Damascus road experience (see Acts 9; 22; 26). As a result of that, he did a complete

180-degree turnaround and channelled all his energy and enthusiasm into spreading the gospel.

What can we learn from Paul's story? What can we learn from his travels and his letters? Above all, his enthusiasm is a lesson to all Christians today. We may not have Paul's physical energy or strength, his intellect or literary skills, or his opportunities or support, but we too can serve God with enthusiasm, wherever we find ourselves. We too can put our best into what we do for God, whatever it may be. There is always more we can do, or we can do what we already do better.

If you get the chance to travel in Paul's footsteps across Turkey or Greece, it's worth taking it—and while you're there, read Paul's letters and Acts. You'll find Paul's enthusiasm stimulating and infectious, and a real inspiration to your own faith and action.

Bible study passages

- Acts 9:1–9
- Philippians 3:4–11
- 2 Corinthians 11:21–29

Questions for discussion

- What is 'enthusiasm'?
- What can be learnt about Paul's faith from his letters?
- What can be learnt about Paul's faith from his travels?
- Discuss the ways in which you have shown enthusiasm for your faith.
- What are the strengths and drawbacks of fanaticism?

Further reading

Stephen W. Need, *Paul Today: Challenging readings of Acts and the Epistles* (Rowman and Littlefield, 2007)
Walter Wangerin, *Paul: A Novel* (Lion, 2001)

16

St George's Day: slaying your dragons

St George's Day on 23 April provides an opportunity to pause and consider the message of this famous third-century saint for us today. Patron saint of England as well as other nations, George is the well-known saint to whom many an English church, school, hospital, cathedral or pub is dedicated. You might easily see 'The George and Dragon' pub in any English village. St George and England go together and the St George flag, a red cross on a white background, is part of the Union Jack.

However, there are so many conflicting stories and legends about George that it's difficult to get to the truth about him. We can't even be sure exactly how many Georges there were. Both Western and Eastern churches recognise St George and he is also known in Islam. He has played such a key part in English life and culture that people often assume he was English, but he wasn't. He simply became popular in England during the Crusader period and ended up as patron saint of the country. He is always pictured with the dragon he traditionally killed.

One version of the story is that George was a soldier who came from Cappadocia in modern Turkey. However, it's also possible that he came from Lydda (modern Lod, near Tel Aviv in Israel) in Palestine. In the sixth century, there was a Byzantine church dedicated to St George in Lydda, and a modern church is there today, where George's tomb can be visited. It's possible that George was a Christian who travelled to Cappadocia when he joined the Roman army. He soon became quite prominent in the army but fell foul of the authorities, who wanted him to sacrifice to the Roman gods. Christianity was still illegal at the time and, when George refused to acknowledge the Roman gods, he was martyred.

The story of George's association with a dragon isn't known until much later. It appears in the medieval work known as *The Golden Legend*.[4] Written by Jacobus de Voragine, Archbishop of Genoa, this book contained stories about many of the Christian saints. The story of George is that while he was in Cappadocia in the service of the Roman authorities, a dragon came into town and settled near the lake. It was a poisonous creature that spat at people who got in its way. In order to calm the dragon, locals offered it sheep to eat, but when it grew tired of sheep, only a young girl was acceptable to it.

The locals cast lots for a victim and the governor's daughter was chosen to be offered to the dragon. At this point George intervened and killed the dragon. He was immediately hailed as a hero and hundreds of locals converted to Christianity and were baptised.

The legends about George spread rapidly and he gradually made his way into mosaics, frescoes, icons and paintings in churches all over the world. In the Muslim communities of the Holy Land today, he is known as *Al Kadre* (the Green) and has a tomb in Beit Jala, near Bethlehem. For both

Christians and Muslims, he is a figure who fights evil and disease.

The story of George and the Dragon is ultimately a story about the defeat of evil. It has sometimes been connected to the dragon (representing Satan) in Revelation 12, which is also concerned with the war between good and evil. In slaying the dragon, George slew the source of evil in that place. Whatever the pedigree of the stories, they form a timeless myth of the triumph of good over evil, and this explains why the story of George and the Dragon has proved so popular in many different cultures of the world.

The defeat of evil by St George brings to mind Jesus' own battles with evil in the Gospels. Mark's Gospel especially presents Jesus as one who is constantly doing battle with the powers of evil. In the early chapters, Jesus encounters demon-possessed people. The demons immediately know who he is and despise him (Mark 1:24). In most of Jesus' healing stories in Mark, he is fighting evil. When he heals the man with the withered hand in Capernaum (3:1–6), when he casts out demons from the man called Legion (5:1–20) or when he's healing nature by stilling a storm (4:35–41), Jesus is fighting the destructive powers of evil. We might also think of John's Gospel, where evil is represented by darkness (1:1–18). The power of darkness is a strong theme in this Gospel and the image appears a number of times (see, for example, 8:12). We're told in the opening section, the Prologue, that 'the light shines in the darkness, and the darkness did not overcome it' (1:5). Again, like George fighting the dragon, Jesus fights darkness in the name of light.

The story of George and the Dragon, connected as it is theologically with Jesus' own purpose, invites us into our own struggle with destructive powers today, although this may not be in ways that we immediately think of. Some of us, of course, might be involved in ministries of exorcism; some might be fighting the evils of injustice and prejudice; some might be fighting poverty and hunger, loneliness and broken relationships or unemployment and social deprivation. But there's another dragon that should also be fought—the one in our own hearts, which is the dragon of selfishness and pride, greed and self-indulgence, arrogance and domination. This personal dragon also needs defeating.

Whatever its status historically, the story of St George and the Dragon calls us to kill our own dragons, eliminate our own poison and slay our own destructive powers. The story challenges us to make personal decisions to reject evil. We can then help others to slay their dragons and thus begin to change our communities and societies at a very basic level. The story of England's patron saint George and the Dragon remains a powerful reminder for us today that there are many evils in our world that need destroying before the kingdom of God can be established.

Bible study passages

- Psalm 74:12–17
- Mark 5:1–20
- Revelation 12:7–12

Questions for discussion

- What are your feelings about the story of St George and the Dragon?
- Does it matter if the stories about St George are true or not? Give reasons.

- What experiences of destroying evil have you had?
- What are the personal 'dragons' you might want to kill?
- How should we understand martyrdom in today's church?

Further reading

David Farmer, *The Oxford Dictionary of Saints* (OUP, 2004)
Craig Hovey, *To Share in the Body: A theology of martyrdom for today's church* (Brazos Press, 2008)

17

Mary, mother of Jesus: pointing to God

Michelangelo's *Pietà* is one of the most beautiful and famous pieces of art in the world. It stands just inside St Peter's Basilica in Rome. In glorious white marble, sculpted in the 15th century when the artist was only 24, the statue depicts Mary in a sitting position, nursing the body of her dead son, Jesus. Not long after the work was completed, there was a dispute about who the sculptor was, so Michelangelo carved his name on Mary's sash: it's the only one of his works to be signed. The statue has had an eventful life over the years. After being moved about in the basilica quite a bit, it travelled to New York in 1964 for the city's World's Fair. In 1972, back in St Peter's, a tourist attacked it with a hammer so it is now protected by a glass case.

Pietà means 'pity' in Italian, so the statue portrays Mary's pity at the death of her son. The theme has been widespread in Christian art and there are many *Pietàs* by different artists, but the one by Michelangelo is the most famous. Mary is portrayed as very young, and there is a moving sense of her love and grief as she holds the dead Jesus in her arms. Most statues of Mary holding Jesus are evocative but this one exudes a unique aura. It breathes a sense of Mary's motherhood, of her love in giving birth to and nurturing her son, but there is also the sense of her grief at his death and of her painful willingness to let him go. As with most statues of the Virgin Mary and child, so with this most sublime *Pietà*, Mary points to Jesus and ultimately to God.

With all its beauty and depth, Michelangelo's *Pietà* raises the question of Mary's place in Christian faith and theology today. There's no doubt that Mary has spoken to millions of people over the centuries and touched the hearts and lives of Christians across a very wide variety of cultures. She is portrayed not only in statues but also in frescoes, mosaics and icons all over the world. Christians flock to shrines such as Lourdes, Fatima, Medjugorje and Walsingham to honour Mary, but she has been the subject of many controversies arising from different beliefs about her. She plays an important part in Orthodox and Catholic Christianity, but far less in Protestantism. How might Christians think of Mary today and what is her place in Christian faith?

First, although not prominent in the New Testament, Mary plays a significant part there. We first meet her at the annunciation, when the angel Gabriel appears to her, announcing that she will give birth to Jesus (Luke 1:26–38). Then comes the visitation, when she goes to stay with Elizabeth (vv. 39–45) and the birth of Jesus (Matthew 1:18–25; Luke 2:1–20). She visits Jerusalem with her family when Jesus is twelve (Luke 2:41–51), is mentioned with other family members in Mark 6:1–6 and is involved in Jesus' first miracle in Cana of Galilee (John 2:1–12). She is at the crucifixion with the beloved disciple (John 19:25–27) and appears again in Acts 1:14, in Jerusalem after the ascension of Jesus. Some commentators think the woman with the moon under her feet in Revelation 12:1–6 might be a representation of Mary.

Over the centuries, Mary's importance in Christian theology, spirituality and devotion grew enormously. She was, of course, respected as the mother of Jesus from the beginning, but she soon became an example of discipleship for Christians because of her response to God's call. Her purity as a virgin also inspired many. Hymns and poems were written in her honour and churches were dedicated to her. At the council of Ephesus in 431, she was affirmed as *theotokos*, meaning 'God bearer' or 'mother of God'. As Jesus was thought of as the 'new Adam' in the New Testament (see 1 Corinthians 15:45), so from the second century onwards Mary was thought of as the 'new Eve'.

In many of the images of Mary holding Jesus, she is clearly pointing to him or displaying him to onlookers. In the Orthodox churches, icons frequently depict Mary holding Jesus, and one of the most important themes in Orthodox iconography is Mary as 'the one who points the way' to Jesus, the emphasis being on Jesus rather than Mary. In the Roman Catholic Church, the dogmas of the Immaculate Conception (1854) and the Assumption (1950) emphasise Mary's place in God's scheme of salvation. Some of the titles of Mary from the second Vatican Council have become popular among Roman Catholics since then: she is 'Mother of the Church' and 'Mother of Christians', but it is maintained in all this that she points to Jesus rather than to herself. Her own words at the wedding feast in Cana, 'Do whatever he tells you' (John 2:5), sum up the significance of Mary as one who leads us towards Jesus.

Michelangelo's *Pietà* is one of the most amazing pieces of art in the world, with iconic status among Christians and art lovers. As with all statues of this type, it shows Mary pointing to Jesus rather than to herself. She points to him spiritually and theologically, as well as physically, but above all she points to God in her motherhood. Our mothers give us life; we grow physically in their bodies. They nourish and nurture us, bringing us up and providing for our needs until they let us go.

Through Mary's motherhood we learn something important about the nature of God. Her motherhood as depicted in the *Pietà* shows us something of how God is with the world he loves and with the creatures he has created. Ultimately, Michelangelo's beautiful statue of Mary and Jesus in St Peter's, Rome, points through them both to God's own love for his children: he loves and nurtures them, and lets them go in freedom.

Bible study passages

- Isaiah 7:10–17
- Luke 1:46–55
- John 2:1–11

Questions for discussion

- What is most important about Mary for Christians?
- How important is Mary in the New Testament?
- What can be learnt from Mary as mother?
- What sort of 'theology of Mary' should Christians have?
- What is the place of Mary in Christian worship?

Further reading

Donald Bolen and Gregory Cameron (eds), *Mary: Grace and hope in Christ* (Continuum, 2006)

Jaroslav Pelikan, *Mary through the Centuries: Her place in the history of culture* (Yale University Press, 1996)

18

All Saints Day: humility and service

Residents of Southampton know all too well that their local football team is known as 'the Saints'. The well-known song 'O when the saints go marching in' is often sung for the team, both at home and away. The mere sound of the song can bring the team to mind, but in fact it has nothing to do with Southampton or with football. It was originally a gospel hymn from New Orleans, used at jazz funerals. It was played as a dirge (at a very slow speed) as the body of the dead person was taken to the grave to be buried. It might be sung again, slightly more quickly, as mourners left the grave after the burial, in the hope that the deceased was indeed now 'marching in' to heaven.

The hymn uses well-known apocalyptic imagery from the book of Revelation. Subsequent verses include the words 'And when the sun refuse to shine'; 'And when the moon turns red with blood' (6:12); 'And when the trumpet sounds its call' (8:1–13); 'And when the new world is revealed' (ch. 21). It conjures up a picture of those who are to enter heaven 'marching in' through the pearly gates. Popularised by Louis Armstrong, Fats Domino and others in the 20th century, the song gradually lost its religious meaning, but even with its original meaning the hymn gives a misleading impression, for 'saints' are not simply those who are marching into heaven at the last opportunity. The training starts much earlier in life, long before we reach the grave. All Saints Day invites us to consider who the saints are and what makes them saints.

Normally, when we think of the saints, we call to mind great names such as the Gospel writers Matthew, Mark, Luke and John, or the disciples Peter, Andrew, James and John. Then there are Paul, the famous apostle to the Gentiles, and his colleague Barnabas, Mary the mother of Jesus, and Stephen the first martyr. Later there are Athanasius, Augustine, Pope Leo and the monastic figures such as Francis, Benedict and Dominic. Augustine of Canterbury brought the Christian faith to Britain in the sixth century and, after the period of the Crusades, George became patron saint of England. Other national patrons are Andrew of Scotland, David of Wales and Patrick of Ireland. In the Orthodox Church, even Old Testament characters such as Moses and Elijah are saints, and we must remember the women—Lucy, Barbara, Anne and Cecilia, the patron saint of music. All of them lived exemplary lives of service and humility.

Many Christians through the centuries were killed because of their faith or were famous examples as teachers and leaders. Not all saints were martyrs, however, and not all martyrs became saints. Some of the greatest Christian martyrs of the 20th century can be seen depicted in stone on the west front of Westminster Abbey, although they are not all saints— the Grand Duchess of Moscow, Martin Luther King, Oscar Romero, Dietrich Bonhoeffer and Maximilian Kolbe. These 20th-century martyrs are certainly of the calibre of the saints. Of course, there are also hundreds of other people who died for their faith or lived for it and remain unknown to us. They should also be remembered on All Saints Day.

What is a saint? Not just someone who's 'marching in' to heaven, and not even someone who has died for their faith. The Christian Church over the centuries has put the saints into stained-glass windows, but it is time to take them out and acknowledge that their saintliness is not to do with abstract piety, being removed from the world. Rather, their holiness and saintliness has to do with the difficult lives they lead. They are not primarily citizens of another world; they are citizens of this one. The saint is usually defined as an example of godly living, as someone to be followed—a teacher, wonder-worker, intercessor or ascetic. Above all, the saint is someone who gives us a glimpse of God, someone who shows God or mirrors God to us in some way. The saint is someone who lives a life of humility and service and reveals God to other people in doing so.

A good Gospel reading for All Saints Day, then, is the Sermon on the Mount. The vision of heaven in the book of Revelation isn't enough; the example of living reflected in Matthew 5:1–12 is crucial too. The 'blessed' there are not particularly pious. They are the 'poor in spirit', those who mourn, the meek, those who hunger and thirst for righteousness, the merciful, the pure in heart, the peacemakers and those who are persecuted. The emphasis in Matthew is on those who are lowly and poor, persecuted and hungry for righteousness. These are the ones who are truly blessed and, indeed, these are the real saints, the holy ones of God. In the New Testament, Paul often calls the followers of Jesus 'the saints', meaning the holy ones in a particular community. They are the ones whose lives are rooted in Christ. The 'blessed' of Matthew 5 are also the holy ones, those who lead a life of service and humility.

The message of All Saints Day is simple: we too can 'go marching in' to the heavenly place to be with God when our time comes, but not by simply turning up at the last minute. There's a price tag attached to becoming a saint, a life to be lived, and that life is one of humility and service, of identifying with the poor and the lost, the search for righteousness and peace. Only those who live out the ethical standards of the Sermon on the Mount can enter the heavenly gathering glimpsed in the book of Revelation. Of course, we all want to be 'in that number' of those who go marching into the heavenly court at the end of time but it's important to start training now.

Bible study passages

- Isaiah 52:13—53:12
- Matthew 5:21–48
- Luke 6:20–38

Questions for discussion

- Who is your favourite saint and why?
- What, in your view, are the marks of a saint?
- Is it harder to live for your faith or die for it?
- Who do you think would qualify as a 21st-century saint?
- What do you understand by Christians 'going to heaven'?

Further reading

David Farmer, *The Oxford Dictionary of Saints* (OUP, 2004)
Jane Shaw, *Practical Christianity: Transforming our lives* (SPCK, 2012)

Festivals

19

The Annunciation: fearing God

The feast of the Annunciation to Mary falls on 25 March and celebrates the appearance of the angel Gabriel to Mary, announcing that she will conceive and bear a son and call him Jesus. It is known as the 'Annunciation to Our Lady' or the 'Annunciation of Our Lord'. The date of the feast is significant: it's nine months before we remember the birth of Jesus on 25 December. The celebration goes back to the eighth century in the West and possibly to the fifth century in the East. As the announcement of the conception of Jesus in Mary's womb, it's a feast of the incarnation, directly related to Christmas.

The story of the annunciation is found only in Luke's Gospel and the event took place in Nazareth of Galilee (Luke 1:26–38). It has been one of the main themes in Christian art over the centuries and there are numerous paintings of it—for example, those by Fra Angelico and Piero Della Francesca in Florence. The National Gallery in London has paintings of the annunciation by Duccio, Lippi and Poussin, among others. There are two important aspects to this feast: first, the event is a theophany or appearance of God through the angel Gabriel, and second, Mary responds with fear.

Luke writes that when the angel Gabriel announces to Mary that she will bear a son, Mary is 'much perplexed'. The angel says to her, 'Do not be afraid, Mary, for you have found favour with God' (vv. 29–30). Later in the conversation, when the son to be born has been described, Mary expresses something of her confusion: 'How can this be, since I am a virgin?' (v. 34). The angel replies that the Holy Spirit will come upon Mary and the Most High will overshadow her. He adds, 'For nothing will be impossible with God' (v. 37). Mary then responds affirmatively, 'Here am I, the servant of the Lord; let it be with me according to your word' (v. 38). She has agreed to participate in the divine plan that has been presented to her: she has said 'yes' to God and agreed to do his will. She has responded positively to what God has asked of her, but she is still perplexed, fearful and troubled; one might even say frightened or disturbed.

Today we don't usually think of fear or disturbance in relation to encountering God. We might use the expression 'He put the fear of God into me' but we don't expect to experience fear when we experience God. Joy, yes! Peace, yes! Awe and wonder, yes! But fear? Of course, there are different meanings of the word 'fear'. Among the many translations of Luke's Greek words describing Mary's reaction here, in addition to 'much perplexed' are 'deeply troubled', 'greatly troubled', 'startled' and 'confused and disturbed'. Certainly we are to think of an experience of awe so great that it could be said to be unsettling. Perhaps there is a sense of being overwhelmed rather than of being frightened.

In the Old Testament there's often fear when God appears. Hagar expresses surprise that she's still alive after an angel has appeared to her (Genesis 16:13). Abram falls on his face when God appears to him (17:3). Manoah's wife sees an angel whom she describes as having an awe-inspiring appearance, like God (Judges 13:6). We know from the psalmist that 'the fear of the Lord is the beginning of wisdom' (Psalm 111:10; see also Proverbs 1:7) and that 'the Lord takes pleasure in those who fear him' (Psalm 147:11). The writer of the book of Proverbs says that 'the fear of the Lord is hatred of evil' (8:13). The writer of Ecclesiastes says, 'Fear God, and keep his commandments; for that is the whole duty of everyone' (12:13). The same emphasis can be found in the prophetic literature of the Old Testament: Isaiah links fear of God with wisdom and understanding (11:2–3) while Jeremiah laments his people's lack of fear of God (2:19).

Fear can also be found in the New Testament. In Acts, the first Christians live 'in the fear of the Lord' (9:31), and Paul can be found, in his letter to the Philippians, encouraging 'fear and trembling' among Christians because God is at work in them (2:12–13). Already at the beginning of Luke's Gospel, Zechariah is terrified and overtaken by fear when Gabriel appears to him in the temple in Jerusalem (1:12). Perhaps the author of the epistle to the Hebrews sums it all up when he says, 'It is a fearful thing to fall into the hands of the living God' (10:31). Mary's fear when the angel Gabriel appears to her, therefore, isn't particularly surprising.

What can we learn from Mary's perplexity and fear? Surely that it is reverence in the face of the overwhelming presence of God. A sense of awe and wonder strikes Mary, a sense of humility in response to God's troubling presence. It's 'troubling' because it is so great, perhaps even 'disturbing'. It challenges her and moves her forward. It asks something new of her. She responds to the angel's message with humility and readiness.

There are many different ways in which God appears to us and many different ways in which we might react. When we encounter the tremendous mystery of God, described by the German philosopher-mystic Rudolph Otto (1869–1937) as the 'numinous', we might well feel fear. We might experience joy, tenderness, peace and goodwill, love and forgiveness, but, like Mary, we might also experience a disturbing fear. When we experience the overwhelming presence of God in our lives, we should not be surprised at such fear. We can respond to it with Mary's courage and readiness to do God's will. That's the most important lesson we can learn from the feast of the annunciation: the realisation of the enormity of God's presence among us and the importance of being ready to do his will in humility and 'fear of the Lord', just as Mary did.

Bible study passages

- Genesis 16:1–16
- Luke 1:26–38
- Hebrews 10:26–31

Questions for discussion

- Describe a time when you felt unsettled in the presence of God.
- In what ways, if any, have you experienced fear in God's presence?
- Why do you think Mary was fearful when she heard the angel's message?

- How important is it to feel at peace in the presence of God?
- In what ways have you responded to a call from God?

Further reading

Eugene LaVerdiere, *The Annunciation to Mary: A story of faith. Luke 1:26–38* (Liturgy Training Publications, 2004)
Tom Wright, *Luke for Everyone* (SPCK, 2001)

20

Mothering Sunday: the motherhood of God

Mothering Sunday is a day for celebrating motherhood and giving thanks for our mothers. On this day we reflect on the place and importance of our mothers in our lives and thank them for everything they've given us. Everyone has (or has had) a mother and today is the day to say a special 'thank you' to her or for her. If your mother isn't living near you, ring her up on this day and say 'thank you', and if she's gone on ahead of us, say a quiet 'thank you' to God in your heart for the blessing of your mother.

It's difficult to think of the best words to sum up our mothers, isn't it? Hopefully, the words are to do with being life-giving, loving and nurturing. They give us warmth, growth, security and a place to feel at home. They're always there for us and can always be trusted. For anyone who hasn't had a good experience of their mother, remember at least that it is their bodies that we have come from and they who provided the wombs in which we grew. Mothering Sunday is a day to remember all this and be thankful.

There are other things we can learn about motherhood, too.

If you go to Norwich, you can visit the cell of Mother Julian, the 14th-century anchoress or hermit who, during a period of great illness, received a series of revelations or 'showings', which she later wrote about in her book *Revelations of Divine Love*. This book is thought to be the first ever written in English by a woman, and Julian has become well known as one of the great English mystics.

To visit her cell and to read her book is to learn a great deal about her understanding of God. Focusing on sinful humanity and our need of God, she writes about the nature of divine love found in suffering and refers several times to God as our mother. This idea is unfamiliar to most Western Christians today but it was not new with Mother Julian. The Old Testament refers to God using female images. In the Psalms, for example, we find images of a midwife (22:9) and of a maid's mistress (123:2) used for God. In Deuteronomy, God is the one who gives birth (32:18) and in Isaiah he is a comforter like a mother (66:13). The idea of God as a mother was developed in early Christianity by important theological writers such as Irenaeus in the second century, Origen in the third, and John Chrysostom, Augustine and Ambrose in the fourth.

More surprising, perhaps, is Julian's idea that Jesus is our mother. A hint of this can already be found in Jesus' own image of himself as a mother hen gathering her chicks: 'Jerusalem, Jerusalem, the city that kills the prophets and stones those who are sent to it! How often have I desired to gather your children together as a hen gathers her brood under her wings, and you were not willing!' (Matthew 23:37). The idea of Jesus as our mother grew particularly in the Middle Ages, and it can be found especially in the writings of St Anselm, Archbishop of Canterbury, and in St Bernard of Clairvaux.

It is Julian, however, who brings this idea of Jesus our mother to its fullest expression. She writes that Jesus 'our Saviour himself is our Mother for we are for ever being born of him, and shall never be delivered!' Later she says, 'He is our Mother, Brother and Saviour' and 'The Second Person of the Trinity is Mother.' Julian writes that 'in our Mother, Christ, we grow and develop'. She points out that God is just as much mother as father. God is mother in that we take our nature from her. Julian even says that Jesus defines the notion of motherhood. 'This fine and lovely word,' she writes, 'is so sweet and so much its own that it cannot properly be used of any but him.' She refers to 'our beloved Mother, Jesus' who 'feeds us with himself' by means of the Blessed Sacrament in the Eucharist.[5] There were others who used the mother image, for example, of the Holy Spirit (especially in the Syrian Church) and Julian herself uses the word 'mother' as an image the Church. Of course, Mary is the 'mother of Jesus' throughout the history of Christianity. Very early in Christian history, she was called 'mother of God'.

What, then, is to be learnt from this rich tradition of calling God and even Jesus our mother? Certainly that God is beyond gender, neither male nor female, and that both masculine and feminine language and images can be used of God. To imagine Jesus as mother is an unexpected connection. He was certainly historically male, but Julian and others who are happy to think of Jesus as mother see an important connection between suffering and pain on the one hand and joy and life on the other. The New Testament already uses the image of childbirth in relation to the death of Jesus and the joy it brings (John 16:20–22). It is in pain that a child is born and that the joy of the mother is born. It's our mothers who go through that pain and through whose pain we are born. Thinking of Jesus as mother draws attention to the mystery of new life born out of his suffering.

On Mothering Sunday we pause to give thanks for our mothers and to remember what they have done for us. We also pause to think of the motherhood of God and of Jesus and to thank them for the new life they give us. Our experience of our mothers as loving, kind, reliable, nurturing, life-giving and trustworthy should also be part of our experience of God's reassuring presence with us. The idea that in Jesus' life and death he suffered pain, as a mother suffers pain in childbirth, is also an important part of our understanding of Jesus. So, on this day we not only give thanks for our mothers but we also celebrate the motherhood of God and of Jesus.

Bible study passages

- Isaiah 66:5–14
- Luke 2:41–52
- John 16:20–22

Questions for discussion

- What are your experiences of motherhood?
- What in your opinion are the key features of being a mother?
- How do you feel about calling God or Jesus 'mother'?
- Do you experience God as mother or father? If so, in what ways?
- What are the weaknesses of mother and father language in relation to God?

Further reading

Julian of Norwich, *Revelations of Divine Love* (Penguin, 1998)
William Paul Young, *The Shack* (Hodder and Stoughton, 2008)

21

Corpus Christi: sanctifying matter

A lot of people are familiar with the name of the French Jesuit scientist-priest Pierre Teilhard de Chardin (1881–1955), but few know in any detail what he had to say. Teilhard, as he is often known, was born in the Auvergne region of France and became a very well-known scientist in biology and palae-ontology in the first part of the 20th century, when the theory of evolution was gaining prominence. He joined the Jesuits early in his life and forged an important connection in popular thinking between science and religion, particularly evolution and the 'cosmic Christ'. For Teilhard, the process by which the material world was 'evolving into consciousness' was fundamentally linked with God and Christ, whom he saw as present in creation in the process of the sanctification or divinisation of material or matter.

Teilhard spent a significant part of his life in China and on one occasion, while out hiking in the Ordos desert, he wanted to celebrate Mass but had no bread or wine. He decided that the whole world would be his altar and that he would offer the sufferings of the world as the elements of the Mass. He later wrote up a meditation on this experience, called 'The Mass on the world'.[6] In it, he says he wants to raise himself up beyond the symbols of the Mass, seeing connections not only between the Eucharist and the cosmos but also between the Eucharist and the sufferings of the world.

One of Teilhard's best-known works is *Le Milieu Divin* or *The Divine Milieu*.[7] The title itself indicates his belief in God's continuing presence in the material world. Indeed, much of his thinking can be summed up in the idea of the sanctification of matter. He saw a fundamental connection between the material world and the Eucharist: just as matter, or bread and wine, are consecrated and sanctified in the Eucharist, so the material world of creation can be consecrated and sanctified, and so can the lives of human beings.

The feast of Corpus Christi, usually observed on the Thursday after Trinity Sunday, has been celebrated in the Western Church since the 13th century. It began with the visions of Juliana of Liege, an Italian woman who supported devotion to the Blessed Sacrament and lobbied for 20 years to get a special day established for it. In the meantime, a priest called Peter of Praga made a pilgrimage to Rome to offer special prayers because he couldn't believe in transubstantiation, the recently articulated Catholic doctrine of Christ's real presence in the Mass. On the way back, he stopped at Bolsena and during Mass, tradition says, the host (the wafer) on the altar bled so much that the corporal (a piece of cloth) became soaked. Pope Urban IV was staying at nearby Orvietto at the time and, when he heard what had happened, asked that the corporal be taken to the cathedral there. In 1264 he established the feast of Corpus Christi as a special devotion to the Blessed Sacrament. Orvietto soon became the focus of festivities on the annual feast of Corpus Christi, and the corporal remains in the cathedral there today.

Of course, Maundy Thursday in Holy Week is the main feast of the Blessed Sacrament. It is the feast of the inauguration of the Eucharist recalling the Last Supper, the meal Jesus ate with his disciples in Jerusalem the night before he died. With the emphasis of that week and that day on the suffering and coming death of Jesus, however, it was thought that a separate day for devotion to the Blessed Sacrament was desirable. Corpus Christi is a feast of the Roman Catholic Church and is not officially observed in the Church of England, although some Anglicans do celebrate it. In 1970 it was broadened to include devotion to Christ's blood and is now called the feast of The Most Holy Body and Blood of Christ.

The important question for us today is this: what can we learn from the feast of Corpus Christi? What is its message? It's important to appreciate not only the significance of the Blessed Sacrament in Christian life and devotion but also its connection with the material world and the whole of creation. On Corpus Christi the focus is on God's transformation of the bread and wine of the Eucharist but we should also remember that God sanctifies all matter throughout creation. The feast reminds us, therefore, that all material can be consecrated and that the whole material world is evolving into its fullness as part of the life of God. Indeed, this is the meaning of the incarnation of God in Jesus: God enters matter and comes to us through matter. He sanctifies matter through his presence in it.

Teilhard de Chardin had a remarkable life. He wrote many books and many have been written about him. He provoked various reactions during his lifetime, not least within the Roman Catholic Church, but his perceptions of God and Christ in creation have special significance in these days when even Christians often forget the connections between faith and the rest of life. Teilhard's message is far-reaching: nothing in the material world is alien to God's sanctifying presence. The scientist-priest teaches us that whatever is occupying us, whether at home or at work, in politics or education, social work or psychology, helping the homeless, hungry or terminally ill; whether on the railways or in car manufacturing, working for the environment or in construction, as artists, musicians or athletes—none of it is outside God's concern as he draws creation to its fullness. The possibility of the sanctification of the material world lies not only at the centre of Corpus Christi but at the heart of Christianity itself.

Teilhard invites us to move beyond our religious symbols, beyond even our sacraments, and to follow the connections between them and the rest of creation.

Bible study passages

- Exodus 16:1–36
- Isaiah 40:12–23
- John 6:35–51

Questions for discussion

- What are your views of Teilhard's 'Mass on the world'?
- What do *you* think is the relation between science and religion?
- What does 'sanctifying matter' mean?
- In what ways does God will the sanctification of all matter?
- What devotion should there be, if any, to the bread and wine of the Eucharist?

Further reading

Ursula King, *Pierre Teilhard de Chardin* (Orbis, 1999)
Timothy Radcliffe, *Why Go to Church? The Drama of the Eucharist* (Continuum, 2008)

22

Transfiguration: shining with God's love

Wouldn't it be wonderful if the whole world were to shine with the love of God? That sounds idealistic, doesn't it? If anyone actually said that, you might wonder whether they had read the newspapers lately or were at all aware of what was going on in the world. It's just not like that in reality. In fact, things seem to get worse every time we read the newspaper or see the news on TV. 'Dream on,' you might say, 'about God's love! How can it happen?' But it's exactly because of the terrible things that happen in the world that we might say this: wouldn't it be wonderful if the whole world were to shine with God's love? The horrors we see everywhere these days might actually encourage us to hope for the shining of God in the world.

The feast of the Transfiguration of Jesus on 6 August is one of the most important feasts of the church's year. The transfiguration is also one of the most important events of the Gospel narratives, and it has an important message for Christians today. Accounts of Jesus' transfiguration occur in all three Synoptic Gospels (Matthew 17:1–8; Mark 9:2–8; Luke 9:28–36).

Surprisingly, though, it's not in John. It occurs in the Synoptics more or less at the centre of the narratives and plays an important part in the disciples' perception of who Jesus is. After his question to them in the region of Caesarea Philippi, 'Who do people say I am?' Jesus goes with his inner group of disciples (Peter, James and John) up a mountain and is transfigured or 'metamorphosed' before them. His face and garments appear shining white. The words 'metamorphosis' and 'transfiguration' refer not only to the disciples' understanding of Jesus but also to his own identity and mission: it's the beginning of Jesus' journey towards death. The theme of the transfiguration of suffering points forward to his resurrection.

The scene on the mountain of transfiguration is reminiscent of other mountain scenes in the Bible, especially Mount Sinai, where the law was given to Moses (Exodus 24; and 33—34). In fact, the Gospel accounts of the transfiguration are based on the encounters that Moses had with God on that mountain. Moses was not allowed to see God's face (33:20) but the law was given and the covenant with the people of Israel was established. The story is clearly a 'theophany' or 'appearance of God'. Mount Sinai (also known as Horeb) is also the mountain where Elijah heard God's 'still small voice' (1 Kings 19:12, RSV). It isn't surprising, then, that Moses and Elijah both appear in the story of the transfiguration. They symbolise the law and the prophets, and what happens to Jesus in the story symbolises his fulfilment of their prophetic roles. There are minor differences of detail between the accounts in Matthew, Mark and Luke but the thrust is much the same: Jesus appears in a new light in relation to what has happened and what will happen to him.

From the early Christian centuries onwards, the transfiguration was remembered by pilgrims to the Holy Land.

It was remembered at Mount Hermon, close to Caesarea Philippi, with its snow-covered peak, and it was remembered at the Mount of Olives in Jerusalem. By the fourth century, however, it was remembered mostly at Mount Tabor in the Jezreel Valley, where it is still commemorated today. There, in 1924, a large church was built by the well-known Italian architect Antonio Barluzzi. There is also a small Orthodox church on the summit of the mountain, which stands at over 1800 feet above the valley, as the transfiguration has been particularly central to theology and spirituality in the Orthodox churches. Anyone familiar with icons will know that among the many themes that appear in them, the transfiguration of Jesus is one of the most important. Icons of the transfiguration usually show the mountain, the disciples and then Jesus at the centre with a shining face and garments.

For the early Christians and still today for Orthodox Christians especially, the transfiguration is not just 'about Jesus'. It's connected to creation in a very important way. Jesus is not just the 'historical Jesus' but the 'cosmic Christ' (that phrase of Teilhard de Chardin). What happens to him has significance for the whole of humanity and the whole of creation. The belief that Jesus was transfigured means that all creation can be transfigured. It's a vision of God's shining presence not just in the face and garments of Jesus himself but throughout the whole of creation.

It's important to emphasise the full significance of the theology of the transfiguration. 6 August is not only the feast of the Transfiguration of Jesus. It's also the anniversary of the dropping of the atomic bomb on Hiroshima in 1945. It's as if we are confronted on this day with two ultimate possibilities for our world: on the one hand, we can opt for evil and destruction; on the other hand, we can opt for working towards

God's transfiguring love in our lives and communities. We can opt for Hiroshima and its destruction or for a world, a creation, a universe, where God's love shines brightly among us and in which creation moves towards its ultimate fulfilment—towards health, wholeness and fullness. This is creation as God wants it to be: a transfigured world shining with God's love.

The feast of the Transfiguration of Jesus, therefore, invites us to consider the possibility of a transfigured world in which God's love shines everywhere among us. It invites us to play our own part in enabling that world to come about, in spite of what we read in the newspapers and see on the TV. The feast of the Transfiguration is a day of hope and of decision-making for everyone.

Bible study passages

- Exodus 24:1–18
- Exodus 33:7–23
- Matthew 17:1–8
- Mark 9:2–8
- Luke 9:28–36
- 2 Peter 1:16–18

Questions for discussion

- Consider places where you have seen God's love shining.
- What do you find most interesting about the transfiguration story?
- What Old Testament background is there to the story?
- In what ways does God transfigure the world today?
- In what ways is the transfiguration different from the resurrection?

Further reading

Andreas Andreopoulos, *This Is My Beloved Son: The transfiguration of Christ* (Paraclete Press, 2012)
Kenneth Stevenson, *Rooted in Detachment: Living the transfiguration* (DLT, 2007)

23

Remembrance: hoping against hope

Remembrance Sunday is a sombre day. It's the day of the year set aside for remembering all those who died in the two World Wars of 1914–18 and 1939–45. Always held on the Sunday nearest to 11 November, it marks the cessation of violence at the end of World War I and is also known as Armistice Day. The focal moment is the exact time at which that war officially ended—the eleventh hour of the eleventh day of the eleventh month—when two minutes' silence is observed. At the Cenotaph in London, the well-known ceremony is held in the presence of the Queen and the Prime Minister. Wreaths are laid in remembrance, gun salutes are sounded and a single Royal Marines bugler plays the Last Post.

There are numerous other ceremonies that mark the occasion. In towns and villages around the country, people gather at their local war memorials to remember the dead. They gather to remember all those who lost their lives in the World Wars and all wars, and to remember all those who served and survived and all those who served and were maimed. They gather to remember men, women and children everywhere who lived through the wars, those whose names are recorded on the memorials and in books of remembrance and those whose names will never be known. On this day, people around the country and around the world remember their lost loved ones and look back in sorrow and grief.

Remembrance Sunday isn't only about looking back, though, as important as that is. It's also about looking forward, for war can give birth to hope, the hope that things can be better in the future. The hope with which we look forward isn't just optimism or wishful thinking about what might be. It's not just 'hoping for the best' or being positive when we could be miserable. Hope is a vision of how things might be when all things come to fulfilment. Hope is rooted in faith in God and in a deep trust in his power to transform things. For Christians, hope is also a commitment to a way of life lived in the light of God's purposes in Christ.

Hope is an absolutely central part of the message of the Bible. It's not just theoretical: it's a view of the world and an attitude to life. In the Old Testament, it's rooted in God's ancient promises to his people and involves trusting in God and waiting on his will with patient endurance. The psalmist writes, 'Commit your way to the Lord; trust in him, and he will act' (37:5). Isaiah of Jerusalem tells his people, 'In quietness and in trust shall be your strength' (30:15), and in the many changing circumstances of the ancient Israelites' lives, the prophets encouraged them to have faith and trust in God's saving purposes in the future (Isaiah 25:9; Jeremiah 29:11). All this is part of our faith that God will bring about his purposes in the world at the end of time.

In the New Testament, hope has the same qualities but is now rooted in God's transforming power to bring all things to their fulfilment through the life, death and resurrection of

Christ. The author of the letter to the Hebrews says, 'Now faith is the assurance of things hoped for' (11:1) and that hope is the 'anchor of the soul' (6:19). In 1 Corinthians 13:13, Paul writes of the close connection between faith, hope and love. Indeed, hope is the basis of faith and love. These three are known as the 'theological virtues' and are central to Christian faith and life.

It isn't that faith and trust in God are always reasonable. Hope isn't just about what will inevitably happen if we wait long enough. In fact, it can be the opposite. In Romans, Paul writes of Abraham's faith, saying that 'hoping against hope' (4:18) he believed and was counted righteous before God. Abraham's faith and trust in God were rooted in a hope that was against all reasonable hope, a hope when hope seemed lost, a hope against simple human hope. That's the sort of hope that inspires and gives life.

The well-known poem by Laurence Binyon, 'For the fallen', written in 1914 and always quoted at the famous Albert Hall poppy service the night before Remembrance Sunday, brings many emotions together on this day:

> *They shall grow not old, as we that are left grow old:*
> *Age shall not weary them, nor the years condemn.*
> *At the going down of the sun and in the morning*
> *We will remember them.*

Less well known are the lines from a previous verse:

> *Solemn the drums thrill: Death august and royal*
> *Sings sorrow up into immortal spheres.*
> *There is music in the midst of desolation*
> *And a glory that shines upon our tears.*[8]

LAURENCE BINYON (1869–1943)

Remembrance Sunday is a day to pause and consider, remember and reflect, and to 'hope against hope'. It's a day of national importance and of personal significance. It's a day when those who don't remember might be reminded and be made aware. It's a day when we look back in loving memory of those who died in war, and around us in sorrow at the way in which war continues in our world. We feel God's glory shining on our tears, and in our loss and grief a new sense of hope is born. In desolation we can hear the divine music playing. As we look back and remember, we also look forward, hoping that God's purposes for a 'new creation' (Galatians 6:15; see Colossians 3:10) might ultimately be realised and that there will be no more war. This is a hope that challenges us to consider what is possible in our world and what must be done in order to achieve it. Remembrance Sunday should remind us all of the hope that people of faith everywhere have—that one day there will be peace on the earth.

Bible study passages

- Jeremiah 17:5–18
- Matthew 28:16–20
- Romans 4:16–25

Questions for discussion

- What experiences of war do you have?
- Can war ever be completely eliminated?
- Why does God allow war?
- What is hope?
- How constructive is it to 'hope against hope'?

Further reading

Jürgen Moltmann, *Theology of Hope* (SCM, 2002)
Tom Wright, *Surprised by Hope* (SPCK, 2007)

24

Harvest: saying 'thank you'

It's always a good idea for parents to teach their children to say 'thank you'. There are particular times when it's appropriate, such as when receiving birthday or Christmas presents or when someone has gone out of their way to be helpful. It's also important in school life where so many fundamental habits and values are learnt. But 'thank you' isn't just for children. Using these important words is a useful habit throughout life, making for good relations with others and nurturing a positive attitude to family and friends and to the world around us. The important thing is this: the habit of saying 'thank you' encourages an 'attitude of gratitude', enabling human flourishing and happiness. Someone might object that you can always say 'thank you' and not mean it or be thankful without saying it, but in the long run, saying 'thank you' helps you really to be thankful and to appreciate what you've been given.

Sadly, in our societies today there's often too little awareness of the basic need to say 'thank you'. Things we need are usually readily available and even gifts can be taken for granted. Possessions and opportunities are often thought of as 'rights' rather than privileges, and a lot of people, adults and children alike, assume that their rights to things prevail over any effort they should make to say 'thank you'. The spin-off is significant: not saying 'thank you' breeds a negative attitude and can reduce someone's sense of the value of life. Where there are no thanks given, there is no appreciation; complacency and indifference prevail.

At Harvest Thanksgiving we say 'thank you' to God for the gifts of the earth, the gift of other people, the gift of life itself and all the blessing we receive. Churches are usually decorated with beautiful flowers and with varieties of food. It's easy to appreciate the beauty of creation in a rural setting. In towns and cities we often feel further away from the 'natural world', but it's all part of creation and we should always maintain the spirit of gratitude. Thanksgiving forms part of our life as human beings and as Christians, and it's not only part of our life together but also part of our worship of God.

Thankfulness is one of the main themes of the Bible, in both the Old and the New Testaments. In the life of ancient Israel, prayers of thanksgiving were offered on a number of different occasions. There were basic thank offerings (Leviticus 7:11–15), as well as thanksgivings on occasions of release from danger or trouble, from hostilities of various kinds and from affliction and death (Psalm 107:17–22). Sacrifices were also offered in thanksgiving (2 Chronicles 33:16) in the temple in Jerusalem and in other places. Music was an important part of thanksgiving and, of course, both thanksgiving and music were important parts of worship (1 Chronicles 25:3). Thanksgiving can be seen especially in the book of Psalms. In Psalm 118:1, for example, we read, 'O give thanks to the Lord, for he is good; his steadfast love endures forever!' The same spirit of thanksgiving can be found in Psalm 136:1.

In the New Testament, Jesus gives thanks at the feedings of the 4000 and 5000 (Mark 8:6; John 6:11) and at the Last

Supper (Mark 14:22–25; 1 Corinthians 11:23–26). Paul often talks about thanksgiving, for example in Philippians 4:6: 'Do not worry about anything, but in everything by prayer and supplication with thanksgiving let your requests be made known to God' (see also 1 Corinthians 14:16; 2 Corinthians 9:11–12). Again, we read, 'But thanks be to God, who in Christ always leads us in triumphal procession' (2 Corinthians 2:14), and finally, 'Thanks be to God for his indescribable gift!' (9:15). In the book of Revelation the 24 elders sitting on their thrones offer thanksgiving to God (11:17).

One of the best-known saints of the Christian Church is Francis of Assisi (1181/2–1226). His feast day falls around the time of Harvest Thanksgiving, on 4 October. St Francis knew how to be thankful and saw the whole of creation as a gift from God. He wrote against the Cathars, a Gnostic sect of his day, who saw the material world as inferior to the spiritual world. The popular film about Francis, *Brother Sun, Sister Moon* (1972), reminds us of his famous 'Canticle of the Sun' in which he offers prayers of praise and glory to all the creatures of the universe: Brother Sun, Sister Moon, Sister Water and Brother Fire. 'Praise and bless the Lord,' writes Francis. 'Render him thanks. Serve him with great humility.'

Francis knew the beauty and goodness of creation. He knew the opening verses of Genesis, in which God sees the various parts of creation as 'good', and in his own writings Francis saw the whole creation as God's gift, for which human beings should be immensely grateful. But there's more than that: Francis imagined creation itself praising God and saying 'thank you' to him. Each individual flower, bird and person praises God and gives thanks to him when it is being truly what God created it to be.

Harvest Thanksgiving, then, is a special day to remind

ourselves of the importance of saying 'thank you', both to God and to each other, and to remind ourselves always to say these words when we get the chance. It's a good habit, teaching us to join in with all creation in praising God for the gifts we receive. It's an amazing vision to see the whole of creation as a vehicle of gratitude to God, and saying 'thank you' to God at Harvest and developing an 'attitude of gratitude' helps us to keep that vision alive throughout the year.

Bible study passages

- Psalm 100
- Deuteronomy 26:1–11
- Luke 17:11–19

Questions for discussion

- Consider the different ways in which you have said 'thank you' to people.
- Why is saying 'thank you' so important?
- Is it all right to have a 'habit' of saying thank you?
- In what particular ways can we say 'thank you' to God?
- What is your opinion of St Francis' idea that the whole creation is praising God in gratitude?

Further reading

Lawrence S. Cunningham, *Francis of Assisi: Performing the gospel life* (Eerdmans, 2004)

Rowan Williams and Joan Chittister, *For All That Has Been, Thanks: Growing a sense of gratitude* (Canterbury Press, 2010)

25

Christ the King: overcoming suffering

On the feast of Christ the King, at the very end of the church's year, it's useful to note just how many different sorts of crucifix there are. Go into a few different churches in your area and you'll soon see quite a variety. Look also at the different types of cross around people's necks, and crucifixes in homes and schools. Most of them don't portray the reality of crucifixion very well at all. At the time of Jesus, crucifixion was a horrible form of capital punishment, but the crosses and crucifixes we usually see are made of gold, silver or wood and depict nothing of Jesus' suffering. Most of them are shiny and expensive. Crucifixes have figures of Jesus on them, while crosses have none. Sadly, few of them really capture the Christian message of the cross.

Some crucifixes, however, show a horrific scene, with Jesus' flesh torn and blood running. Clearly he is dying a painful and tormenting death, but in these crucifixes there is nothing of the resurrection, so the real Christian message of the cross is still lost. In order to get the right balance, some artists have made or painted what is known as the *Christus Rex* or

'Christ the King' crucifix. There are different types but they usually have some sort of combination of the suffering and rising of Jesus, trying to portray his death and resurrection together as a single reality. On some of them, the obviously suffering Jesus is depicted at some distance from the cross, showing him physically rising. Often a *Christus Rex* depicts Christ wearing eucharistic vestments, indicating a connection with the Eucharist. Each portrayal has its own strengths and weaknesses but the *Christus Rex* portrays Christ as a particular sort of king: his kingliness is related to his death.

How, then, are we to understand the image of Christ as a king? For most people, kings are figures of worldly power. Royalty and monarchy are associated with power and wealth, worldly riches and the domination of subjects. Kings and queens are rulers of the people, usually distant figures who are powerful symbols of state. From ancient Israel, Saul, David and Solomon come to mind. In ancient Egypt there were Pharaohs, such as Tutankhamun and Ramses. From Rome, we think of emperors such as Tiberius, Titus and Trajan, while the Greeks had Alexander the Great. The Byzantine Christian emperors included figures such as Constantine and Justinian. In our own day, kings, presidents and prime ministers all have worldly power and glory.

What about Jesus as a king? In the Old Testament, people already thought of God as a king. Psalm 97 opens with exactly this idea: 'The Lord is king! Let the earth rejoice'. The early Christians soon took the title 'king' and used it of Jesus. He was 'King of the Jews' (Mark 15:2) and was mocked as an earthly king at his trial (vv. 16–20). He preached the kingdom of God, and his parables were parables of that kingdom (1:15; 4:1–33).

In what sense, precisely, is Jesus a king? Not in the worldly sense of power, wealth and distance. We read in John's Gospel that Jesus' kingdom is 'not from this world' (18:36) even though, of course, it has much to do with this world. Jesus is a different sort of king, one whose kingliness is connected to his death, as shown by the *Christus Rex* image. His throne is the cross, and his rule is rooted in humility and death.

It should be no surprise, then, that the Gospel reading chosen for Christ the King Sunday in some churches is the parable of the sheep and the goats (Matthew 25:31–46). The scene is well known: it depicts the end of time, when the Son of Man comes with his angels and sits on his throne of judgment. It's important to note that Jesus the Son of Man is on the throne here, not Jesus the glorious king. In the Gospels, the 'Son of Man' is a name for Jesus that is associated with suffering (see, for example, Mark 8:31). His kingship is founded on his suffering and his death on the cross, and his kingdom consists of those who do what he has himself done. He has healed the sick and lived with the outcast; he has fed the hungry and visited the lost. In Matthew 25 the righteous, or the members of the kingdom, are those who have fed the hungry, given the thirsty a drink, welcomed strangers, clothed the naked and visited those in prison. Jesus' kingship is seen fundamentally in his service of the lost and in his raising of the weak. It's found in his healing and life-giving ministry, and it is ultimately in his humility and death that the light of his resurrection shines, in his lowliness as a human being that his divinity shows through.

Once, when I was asked to give a talk on which is more important, the cross or the resurrection, I stressed that they cannot be separated. They are two sides of a coin, two aspects of a single reality, which should be understood together. Good Friday and Easter Day are one. For this reason, the *Christus*

Rex is surely an excellent rendering of Christ the King. If it portrays the reality of death together with the glory of the resurrection, then it's doing its job. It is keeping the death and resurrection of Jesus in their proper relation to each other, showing them together as a single reality. In the end, Jesus is king not only because he feeds the poor, heals the sick, dies on a cross and overcomes it all in new life; he is king because he walks the path of suffering and triumphs over it.

Bible study passages

- Psalm 93
- Isaiah 6:1–13
- Matthew 25:31–46

Questions for discussion

- What different crucifixes have you seen and which do you prefer?
- In what senses should God be called 'king'?
- In what senses is Jesus a king?
- What are the drawbacks of calling Jesus a king?
- What image is the best one for the power of God?

Further reading

Rowan Williams, *Resurrection: Interpreting the Easter Gospel* (DLT, 2002)
Tom Wright, *How God Became King: Getting to the heart of the Gospels* (SPCK, 2012)

Part Two
Emmaus

God

1

God and the world:
separate or together?

William Blake's best-known painting is probably *The Ancient of Days*. Originally done in 1794 as the frontispiece for one of his illustrated books, it's now in the British Museum. Often reproduced as a popular art poster in recent decades, the work depicts God as an old man in the sky, complete with white hair and beard. He sits in the clouds, leaning down with a compass in his hand, creating the world. The painting takes its title from the book of Daniel where the 'Ancient of Days' is the name for God (7:9). Another of Blake's masterpieces is *Newton as a Divine Geometer* (1795) in which the scientist Isaac Newton sits at the bottom of the sea, marking out creation like God with a compass. Blake's Newton is vividly portrayed in Eduardo Paolozzi's striking bronze sculpture just outside the British Library in London.

These images of creator and creation raise the question of

God's relation to the world. How are we to think of it? Is God far above us, sitting on a cloud, removed from the stuff he creates, as in the book of Daniel, or is he thoroughly involved with the world, interacting with it and intertwined with its growth and development? Sadly, although Blake's intentions were to challenge Newton's idea of the world as a machine and God as distant, these two paintings have often reinforced the idea that God is indeed an 'old man in the sky', distant from creation, intervening only occasionally when needed. It's unfortunate that this distant God is often envisaged by believers and unbelievers alike. In fact, the Christian God is anything but distant and removed: he's involved with creation and creation is involved with him.

In some books of the Bible, God is not a distant figure. He's involved with creation, and human beings come to know him through it. In the book of Genesis, God is a creator who seems to be caught up with what he's creating (ch. 1), and later in the Old Testament his continuing interaction with and concern for the world is stressed. In the Psalms, for example, we read, 'The heavens are telling the glory of God; and the firmament proclaims his handiwork' (19:1), showing that God can be known through creation. Later we read, 'You cause the grass to grow for the cattle, and plants for people to use' (104:14), showing his continuing life-giving presence in creation. In a number of places, God's creation of the world is depicted as a process in which he fights off chaos and evil (for example, Psalm 74:12–17). There is also the sense, especially in the prophetic books, that God's activity in creation continues into the future and brings about a 'new creation' at the end of time (Ezekiel 40—48; Isaiah 40—55).

It's particularly noticeable that the first Christians saw a serious connection between God, Christ and creation. Paul writes that Christ is the 'firstborn of all creation' (Colossians 1:15) and of God 'reconciling the world to himself' in Christ (2 Corinthians 5:19). He says that 'the whole creation has been groaning in labour pains' (Romans 8:22) until the time of Christ and that there is a 'new creation' in Christ (Galatians 6:15; see Colossians 3:10). John's Gospel sees the *Logos*, or Word of God, as his instrument of creation, saying, 'All things came into being through him, and without him not one thing came into being' (John 1:3), and the author of the book of Revelation writes of 'a new heaven and a new earth' (21:1) at the end of time. In many parts of the Bible, then, God isn't a distant figure. He not only creates the world but continues to shape and mould it into its final form by the end of time.

The idea of God's distance from creation grew strong in the 18th century with a group of thinkers known as the Deists. In the light of scientific knowledge and Newton's idea that the world was a machine, they stressed that God had created the world but then withdrawn from it. Deism is now thought of as exactly this belief: God is separate and remote from the world. Like a clockmaker, he leaves the clock to tick on its own and only intervenes when he needs to.

In more recent theology, the notion that God is distant has been seriously challenged, not least by 'process theology'. Following the philosophy of Alfred North Whitehead and Charles Hartshorne, process theologians stress that the world is more like a plant than a clock—not a machine with mathematical rules that govern it, but more of an organic process. The world is an organism in the process of growth that God permeates and influences. The notion of a growing and developing universe has also been stressed in recent scientific thinking, for example, in quantum physics. Here, the world is seen as being made up of *quanta* or bundles of energy. This concept of the world is much more fluid and developmental than Newton's and much closer to the overall biblical view. Scientist-theologians such as John Polkinghorne have done a great deal to break down the barriers between science and religion by seeing God as thoroughly bound up with the evolving physical universe.

William Blake's paintings *The Ancient of Days* and *Newton as a Divine Geometer* were originally intended to counter the idea that God and the world are separate. Blake himself was an unorthodox visionary who saw the divine everywhere in creation. Unfortunately, these paintings have often had the opposite effect, reinforcing the sense of God's distance from the world and of the creator as an 'old man in the sky'. A good deal of Christian experience has actually been the opposite, that while God and the world are not the same thing, they are thoroughly involved with each other. God permeates the world at all times, drawing it to its ultimate completion through his presence in it.

Bible study passages

- Genesis 1:1–31
- Colossians 1:15–20
- Revelation 21:1–27

Questions for discussion

- How have you experienced God seeming especially distant or especially close?
- In what ways would you say God and creation are related to each other?

- What sense does it make to say that God 'influences' creation?
- What does it mean to say that Christ can be known in creation?
- In what ways would you say science and religion are similar or different?

Further reading

Bruce Epperly, *Process Theology: A guide for the perplexed* (T&T Clark International, 2011)

John Polkinghorne, *Quantum Physics and Theology: An unexpected kinship* (SPCK, 2007)

2

Seeing God: a way of life

Where do you 'see God'? Where do you experience God? Where is God most real to you? There are probably particular times in your life when you sense God's presence more than you normally do—special places where you feel close to God. You might have had a particular conversion experience that gave rise to your faith or it might have taken years to feel close to God. It might have been in a blinding light like Paul's experience on the Damascus road (Acts 9:1–9) or in a long, painful process like St Augustine's. In any case there are surely times and places where you feel God's presence breaking into your life more completely, places where you 'see God' more clearly.

You might see God in the beauty of the natural world, looking at a sunset or a landscape. You might sense him in art or music, looking at a particular painting or listening to your favourite symphony. You might feel his presence in literature, poetry, sport or athletics. Even more likely, you will find him in personal relationships and the company of your family. You might see God in the birth of your child and as you watch your children grow up. You might see him in other people as you serve and help them, and you might also find him in your deepest moments of sorrow, during an illness, after an accident or when you've lost someone you love. You might sense God in an uplifting service at church or on a pilgrimage or retreat, or it might simply be in the silence of your own private meditation at home that you find him near. All these times are important for Christian faith. Places, events and people are locations of religious experience and revelation. Yet for Christians there is something even more central than all this: the life of Jesus reveals God to us more deeply than anything else.

In John's Gospel, the disciple Philip asks Jesus to 'show us the Father' in order that he might 'be satisfied' (14:8). He wants to see God in order to satisfy his curiosity. We often make the same request, that God will show himself somehow in our lives to convince us he is real. It's often for our own satisfaction that we want to see God, to put our own fears or doubts to rest or to reassure ourselves that we're on the right track and our faith is not in vain. Non-believers often demand that God 'show himself' in order that they might be convinced of his existence. It's perhaps a natural temptation to want to be sure of God's presence in our lives, but this approach misses the importance of faith and belittles its content. God isn't there simply to be looked at and experienced. He is more a mystery to be entered into than a curiosity to be satisfied.

Philip's request to 'see the Father' follows a very important event that occurs in the previous chapter of John's Gospel. It's the Last Supper, when Jesus washes his disciples' feet in humility and service, foreshadowing his suffering and death. During the meal with his disciples, he lays his garments aside, takes up a towel and washes their feet. His ministry in this and other ways demonstrates the nature of his purpose among them: he comes as a servant, and they are asked to follow the example he gives. Another disciple, Thomas (the one who appears at the end of the Gospel, wanting empirical verification for his faith, John 20:24–29), says that the disciples don't know where Jesus is going. Jesus replies that he himself is the way, the truth and the life (14:6). Jesus asks Philip, 'Have I been with you all this time, Philip, and you still do not know me?' (v. 9). There is something here that the disciples are missing.

Jesus' point is this: he has already shown Philip the Father in his actions and life so far. In particular, Philip should have seen God in the humble actions of service that Jesus has carried out at the Last Supper and elsewhere. 'Seeing God' isn't just a matter of satisfying curiosity. It isn't just about looking at God and expecting a special experience. A deeper insight into the nature of God is possible through seeing the sort of life that Jesus lives. Jesus is showing his disciples a new vision of God in the way he lives, which continues through to his death and resurrection. Philip is missing the point: if he really wants to 'see the Father' he should look at the life of Jesus.

So where do you 'see God'? It may well be in the beauty of creation, in sunsets and long walks in the country. It may be in art and music and special moments of religious experience and revelation. It may be through particular people you know. It will certainly be in the special times and key moments of your life. And, yes, there may be times when you wish you had more certainty of God's presence, when you wish that God felt closer. All this is important in the life of faith, which seeks to grow and to know God ever more deeply.

With Philip, however, we Christians are asked to look beyond satisfying our curiosity. We are asked to go beyond the buzz of a religious experience, to look at the life Jesus lived.

Jesus is 'the way, the truth and the life' because his life reveals what God is like. When we look at his life, we see God in a new way, revealed through lowliness, humility, service to others, death and resurrection, and we too are asked to participate in that way of life. Like Philip, we are invited into a lifestyle that will enable us to see God more clearly. Our vision will then go beyond personal satisfaction: it will be participation in the life of God himself.

Bible study passages

- Psalm 19
- Jeremiah 1:4–10
- Philippians 2:6–11

Questions for discussion

- Discuss your most vivid experience of God's presence.
- Have you had a 'conversion experience' of any sort? If so, what was it like?
- Think of a person who has influenced your faith a lot. What was it about them that influenced you?
- What is it about Jesus' life that reveals God to us?
- What is 'humility'?

Further reading

John Pritchard, *Living Jesus* (SPCK, 2010)
Graham B. Usher, *Places of Enchantment: Meeting God in landscapes* (SPCK, 2012)

3

The big picture:
God and evil

I think most people know the expression 'Keep your eye on the big picture'. Sometimes, when we're getting bogged down in minutiae and arguing about detail, someone says, 'OK, keep your eye on the big picture.' Psychologists tell us there are two kinds of people—'detail' people and 'big picture' people. Being told to 'keep your eye on the big picture' can be annoying if you're a 'detail' person but it can sometimes be important to get a broader perspective on things. In relation to God, it can often be a good idea to ask ourselves what the big picture is and what we think God is doing overall.

The parable of the weeds in Matthew 13:24–30 (explained in verses 36–43) tells of a man who sowed seed in his field. When the seed grew, he found weeds as well: an enemy had got in and sowed them to spoil the crop. The field is the world, the seeds are the children of the kingdom and the weeds are the children of the evil one. The way the parable is interpreted in Matthew indicates that there is both good and evil in the world. This is how things will be until the end of time, when everything will be sorted out. There is one thing the parable doesn't tell us, though: how did the enemy get in? We know that the weeds are not wanted, but how did they get into the field in the first place?' Is the enemy, the devil, a force in his own right or has God allowed him in and, if so, why?

This challenging parable raises the age-old problem of evil and suffering. Why are there evil and suffering in the world and where do they come from? Are good and evil, God and the devil, ultimately two powerful and equal forces in the world? Has God allowed evil into the world for a reason? These questions raise others: in what sense does God have complete control in the world, and what is God's relation to the devil? Christians believe that God is 'almighty'. Anglicans pray, 'Almighty God unto whom all hearts are open...', and in the Creed we say, 'I believe in God the Father almighty...'. In what sense, then, is God 'almighty'? Does it mean that he can do anything he likes and, if so, why doesn't he stop evil and suffering? Philosophers and theologians have speculated about these questions for centuries but the problem remains.

We don't have to look far to see suffering, pain and evil around us. Media reports keep us well informed about the amount of evil in our world. There's so-called moral evil that human beings create (violence, murder, terrorism) and natural evil, for which we are not responsible (earthquakes, famines, floods). If God is almighty and also loving, why does he allow suffering to continue? Why are there so many weeds in the field? Some say that God has given human beings free will so that we can know the difference between good and evil. Even if this is true, though, are we responsible for 'natural evil'?

A lot depends on how you see the 'big picture'. In the fourth century, Augustine, one of the most influential theologians of the Western Church, said that God created the world perfect. It was then spoilt by human beings. 'Original perfection' was ruined by the fall of Adam, which introduced sin and evil into the world. Before Augustine, though, in the second century, Irenaeus had a different view. He thought the world had been created with an 'original innocence'. Rather than being perfect to start with, he claimed, the world grows towards perfection like a child growing up, making mistakes along the way but still moving forward towards a greater degree of perfection. In fact, this view is closer to the biblical view and that of many modern scientists and theologians. The world is basically an organism rather than a machine, growing gradually towards completion. If you look at the 'big picture', you can see the world as God's project, which he is in the process of bringing to perfection. You can then see that there are still important tasks to be done before it reaches its final state.

In the letter to the Romans, Paul talks about the whole creation 'groaning' as it moves forward towards freedom from bondage to decay (Romans 8:22). He says, 'I consider that the sufferings of this present time are not worth comparing with the glory about to be revealed to us. For the creation waits with eager longing for the revealing of the children of God' (vv. 18–19). In this, Paul looks forward to the end of time when God's purposes for the whole of creation will be complete.

It may sound harsh to suggest that we must wait in faith and hope to see what God's ultimate purposes for creation are. It may sound as if we are belittling the suffering, pain and evil in our world, but it is a response which is in tune with biblical and scientific teaching. We must keep our eyes, as far as possible, on God's long-term project of bringing creation to what he finally wants it to be. The evil and suffering in the world will gradually be eliminated in God's plan to heal everything as he draws the whole creation forward towards its final state.

Why are there weeds in the field and why is there evil in the world? In the big picture, it's because God wants to bring his project of creation to a greater perfection than he would be able to do otherwise. It's not that God wants evil and suffering, but that he allows it for the sake of greater healing than would otherwise be the case. The good news is that God transforms evil in the end, when the harvest comes. The weeds will eventually be pulled out and creation will finally be what God intends it to be.

Bible study passages

- Job 1:13–22
- Mark 1:21–28
- Mark 7:24–30

Questions for discussion

- What examples of evil and suffering have you seen?
- What is the difference between evil and suffering?
- Why do you think there are evil and suffering in the world?
- Why does God allow evil and suffering?
- How helpful is the notion that God is gradually drawing creation towards perfection?

Further reading

Chad Meister, *Evil: A guide for the perplexed* (Continuum, 2012)
N.T. Wright, *Evil and the Justice of God* (SPCK, 2006)

4

Faith and doubt: seeking understanding

Richard Holloway's autobiography *Leaving Alexandria: A memoir of faith and doubt* tells the story of the author's life, from his birth and upbringing in Scotland, through his training for the priesthood at the Society of the Sacred Mission at Kelham Hall in Nottinghamshire, his time spent in Ghana, and his ministry as Vicar of Old St Paul's in Edinburgh, Rector of the Church of the Advent in Boston, Massachusetts, Bishop of Edinburgh, and Primus or Archbishop of the Scottish Episcopal Church, to the time when he finally stood down in 2000. He threw his mitre in the Thames, fed up with the church and God and bewildered about what was coming next. Now he walks in the hills in Scotland, still seeking meaning in his life.

More important than all the detail of Holloway's appointments is his struggle with God. Brought up in an Anglo-Catholic church in Scotland, he experienced a powerful and formative monastic training at Kelham, which left a lifelong impression on him. His understanding of his faith was formed through traditional concepts of God and the sacraments of the church, but gradually he became aware of the philosophical problems of religious belief. His everyday experience as a priest confronted him with the problematic issues of life and death and the nature of God and providence. In Boston he learnt about the marginalisation of women and gay people in local communities and the effect this had on the church. Gradually, Holloway came to see that God, if he exists, cannot be fully known. Aware of the deep complexity in the relation between God's presence and absence, he knew that faith and doubt are deeply connected. The problem was to know how.

Most of us probably experience something of the same tension between faith and doubt. We imagine that doubting means falling from faith, and that faith should be crystal clear and for ever the same. Doubt is therefore regarded as failure, a movement away from faith. We become disillusioned when we doubt and think we have 'lost our faith'. For many people, faith is connected with 'belief' and is considered primarily as believing in the truth of religious statements—for example, about God or Jesus. We're often asked, 'Do you believe in God?' meaning 'Do you believe that God exists?' We are asked, 'Do you believe Jesus is the Son of God?', meaning, 'Do you believe that that statement is true?' Belief is connected with intellectual assent and faith is thus thought of in the same terms. Doubt is understood as the opposite of faith: doubting God's existence or that Jesus is the Son of God means that we don't 'believe' it. Some Christians reach crisis point over this experience, while others find themselves on the margins of belief, for the same reason.

However, there's more to it than that. Paul Tillich's book *Dynamics of Faith* is a modern classic with an important message. A German theologian with a notable career in the USA in the last century, Tillich defined faith as 'ultimate concern'. He had been an army chaplain as well as an academic in various universities and had seen a few different sides of life. Our 'ultimate concern', he says, is whatever we are 'ultimately concerned' about. It's the thing that really drives us, that we're most interested in, that we most treasure—the thing we ultimately stand for, whether we know it or not. This idea is reminiscent of Jesus' saying in the Sermon on the Mount, 'Where your treasure is, there your heart will be also' (Matthew 6:21).

For Tillich, our ultimate concerns might be our lives or our careers, our jobs or our bank accounts, our countries or our football teams. It might also be God. If we're ultimately concerned or bothered about it, if it's the thing that, in the end, we are most driven by, then that's our religion, says Tillich. It's not difficult to see that somebody's religion might be their career or their car, their football team or whatever their particular hobby is, but Tillich adds that there is always an element of 'in spite of' about our ultimate concern. We follow the concern 'in spite of' limitations or likelihood of disappointment. We still 'believe in' the cause 'in spite of' the factors stacked against it. In other words, our ultimate concern can be quite irrational.

So it is with our religion and faith. There will always be some factors stacked against it. That's inevitable, but we believe nevertheless. So, Tillich argues, doubt is an important part of faith—it forms part of the dynamics of faith—and he adds that this is where courage comes in as well. By doubt, he doesn't really mean doubting statements of faith as much as having an attitude of doubt. He sees doubt as a healthy part of a searching faith, which helps us seek understanding in our faith, and courage is a kind of 'leap of faith', which must always be there if faith is to be mature and wholesome.

Richard Holloway's autobiography is a reminder of how

faith and doubt go together. We're all struck by doubt occasionally, but this is healthy if it enables us to grow into a deeper relationship with God. Of course, doubt is quite different from lack of interest, or cynicism. People who dismiss religious belief in a cynical manner, with no interest in it, aren't 'doubting' in Tillich's sense. That's something quite different. Interested doubt already shows a degree of involvement with and belief in what is being doubted. It's in that sense that doubt is part of faith.

Anselm of Canterbury (1033–1109) prayed that he might believe in order to understand.[9] This has become known as 'faith seeking understanding' and, if doubt is part of that faith-seeking, our faith will be more mature and more informed. We shouldn't shy away from our doubts but should embrace and explore them, for, in the end, faith and doubt form part of a single quest.

Bible study passages

- Judges 7:1–25
- Mark 5:25–34
- John 20:19–29
- Hebrews 11:1–12

Questions for discussion

- How would you define 'faith'?
- What is 'doubt'?
- Are there times when you have serious doubts? What about?
- To what extent can doubts be opportunities for growth in faith?
- Are we 'losing our faith' when we have doubts?

Further reading

Richard Holloway, *Leaving Alexandria: A memoir of faith and doubt* (Canongate, 2013)
Paul Tillich, *Dynamics of Faith* (HarperCollins, 2001)

5

Treasure:
where your heart is

Like many people, you may have read *Treasure Island* when you were at school. An exciting children's story written by Robert Louis Stevenson in 1883, it's about the search for treasure and has all the hallmarks of a classic adventure story. Today, the tale almost defines the concept of a 'desert island', with its buried treasure and the search for what's hidden there. Over the years, the book has been so popular that numerous films and TV programmes have been based on it.

Treasure Island begins in the south-west of England at an inn called the Admiral Benbow. The narrator of most of the story is the young Jim Hawkins, the son of the owners of the inn. A pirate arrives at the inn with a map of the location of some treasure on an island. The treasure belonged to the late Captain Flint, and before long, some of Flint's opponents also arrive, trying to steal the map and details of the treasure's whereabouts. In the events that ensue, Jim Hawkins manages to get hold of the oilskin map and shows it to a magistrate, Dr Livesey, and his friend Squire Trelawney. They decide to head for the island to find the treasure. They gather a band of men together, including Long John Silver, a one-legged seafaring man with a parrot on his shoulder, and set off on a hired schooner called the *Hispaniola*. Jim Hawkins is also on board.

Soon there's division in the ranks. Long John Silver wants the treasure himself and wins others over to his side, against Livesey and Trelawney. In a famous scene, Jim Hawkins is collecting apples from a barrel and decides to hide there when he hears voices. He overhears Silver's plans to kill his opponents and take the treasure. Hawkins warns Trelawney, and Silver's plan is thwarted. When they finally get to the island, they go to the spot where the treasure should be but find it gone. A man called Benn Gunn, who is marooned on the island, joins with Jim Hawkins in helping Trelawney to prevail over the others. Many are killed and Trelawney wins the day. Ben Gunn has had the treasure in his cave all along and shares it with Trelawney's men. In the end, Long John Silver gets away alive and takes a small portion of the treasure with him. A truly gripping tale, *Treasure Island* has inspired generations of schoolchildren and adults alike.

All of us probably have a sense of the value of treasure and of what we treasure most. It might not only be the hope of getting something valuable in the future, like winning the lottery. Perhaps we treasure an object we already possess— perhaps a gift or something we've won. Our treasure might be a piece of jewellery we've been given, a birthday or Christmas present, or something priceless. It might be an object of sentimental more than monetary value, but it's still our 'treasure', which we would hate to lose. A person—a spouse, parent, son or daughter—could be our treasure. It is something of ultimate value to us, beyond everything else we could ever have or want.

In Matthew 13:44, Jesus tells a parable about a man who

discovers treasure hidden in a field. He covers it up and then, in his joy, goes and sells everything and buys the field. Here the kingdom of heaven is the treasure. It's something so well worth having that the man hides it for a while and then gets rid of everything else so that he can buy the field with the treasure in it. The story is a simple illustration of ultimate value and worth. The treasure is priceless, worth more than anything else to the man. Like him, we might have had the experience of finding treasure: buying things we have wanted for a long time or selling possessions to enable us to get something better. The parable of the treasure reminds us of what is of ultimate worth to us: we will go to any lengths to get it. Jesus' next parable, in Matthew 13:45, the parable of the pearl of great price, has the same message.

So what is your treasure? What is of ultimate value to you? As Christians, our treasure should be the kingdom of God, or the rule of God in our lives. The kingdom of God is like treasure: it should be worth more to us than anything else we could want. It should be worth getting rid of everything to secure it, and the joy that the man in the parable had when he found the treasure should be our joy too when we are in God's presence. Indeed, we should seek nothing else but the presence of God in our lives. We should seek the kingdom of God with the gusto of the pirates in *Treasure Island*. We should guard our life with God as if it were the most valued possession we have. We should seek the field where God dwells and buy it.

In an earlier chapter of Matthew's Gospel, in the Sermon on the Mount, Jesus says, 'Do not store up for yourselves treasures on earth… but store up for yourselves treasures in heaven' and then, 'For where your treasure is, there your heart will be also' (6:19–21). The author of the well-known

Irish hymn 'Be thou my vision' sums it up very well in the penultimate verse of that hymn:

Riches I heed not, nor man's empty praise,
Be thou my inheritance now and always,
Be thou and thou only the first in my heart,
O Sovereign of heaven, my treasure thou art.[10]

TRANSLATED BY MARY BYRNE (1880–1931); VERSIFIED BY ELEANOR HULL (1860–1935)

Bible study passages

- Exodus 32:1–29
- Matthew 6:19–21
- Matthew 13:44–46

Questions for discussion

- What would you define as a treasure?
- Consider times when you have gone to great lengths to get something you treasured.
- What is your ultimate treasure?
- How helpful is it to think of God or the kingdom of God as 'treasure'?
- What should Christians treasure most?

Further reading

Robert Louis Stevenson, *Treasure Island* (Penguin, 2000)
Tom Wright, *Matthew for Everyone: Part 1 Chapters 1—15* (SPCK, 2002)

6

Repentance:
saying you're sorry

One of the most popular songs of the 1970s was 'Sorry seems to be the hardest word' by Elton John and Bernie Taupin. It featured on Elton's *Blue Moves* album and came out as a single in 1976. A great success early on, it later found its way on to all the Elton John *Greatest Hits* and *Very Best of...* albums. It has had a number of different covers over the years, including those by Joe Cocker (1991) and, more recently, Blue (2002). There are versions in different musical genres and different languages and the song became popular again through the album *Good Morning to the Night* by Elton John and Pnau (2012). Whether you like the music or not, the words are striking: they speak of love and a broken relationship, and how difficult it is to say you're sorry.

Most of us know what it's like to feel sorrow. We've said something to our spouse that we wish we hadn't said. We've done something to someone that we wish we hadn't done. Something has occurred that needs an apology but we hesitate to make the move. Then we realise how necessary it is to try to take the road towards making amends. Of course, we might say 'I'm sorry' without meaning it, and we might feel sorry but be unable to say so because of pride, arrogance or weakness. In any case, 'I'm sorry' cannot be words alone but will need putting into action.

When we finally say 'I'm sorry', new possibilities appear in our relationship: it's as if a door opens. Saying you're sorry isn't about the past. It's about the future, about creating a space in which a new relationship can occur, and often the renewed relationship can be better than the original one: there's been breakage and there's been renewal.

The Christian understanding of 'repentance' is about saying we're sorry. The Hebrew and Greek words used in the Old and New Testaments mean 'to turn', 'to turn around' and 'to return'. They signify a change of direction and a commitment to a new path. In the Old Testament prophetic books, the idea occurs often, and it's used in connection with the notion of faith as a journey. The prophets exhort the ancient Israelites to return to the right path. Amos complains that they have not returned to God (4:6–13); Hosea, using the image of the unfaithful wife, says, 'Come, let us return to the Lord (6:1), and Jeremiah adds a personal touch when he speaks of the need for a new covenant in the heart (31:31–34). Ezekiel 33:7–11 speaks of the wicked man turning from his ways, while Psalm 119 says, 'Teach me, O Lord, the way of your statutes' (v. 33) and 'Turn my eyes from looking at vanities' (v. 37). In all these cases, the sense is one of turning towards the path of God, having done something wrong. The contrast is between the way of God and the way of sinners. Change is fundamental and a process of restoration is made possible. 'Sorry' is a crucial word.

In the New Testament, 'sorry' or 'repentance' is equally important. John the Baptist proclaims 'a baptism of repentance for the forgiveness of sins' (Mark 1:4) and, at the beginning of Jesus' ministry, he says, 'The time is fulfilled, and the kingdom of God has come near; repent, and believe in the good news' (v. 15). In his sermon in Acts, Peter says, 'Repent, and be baptised' (2:38). It's clear that, in the New Testament, repentance is related both to sin and to faith. Paul doesn't use the word very much but the idea is important in his theology. At the beginning of Romans (2:4), he says, 'Do you not realise that God's kindness is meant to lead you to repentance?'and it's clear that, for Paul, the response of faith to what God has done for us is 'repentance' (compare Romans 3:25). In all these cases, repentance and faith are about 'turning around' and making a new start. They are about being sorry.

As Christians we are called to repentance, called to 'turn around' and take another path, called to say we're sorry. The Eucharist begins with a confession of sin, which is an opportunity to say we're sorry to God. Such confession and repentance invite us into a change of direction, a return to the path that God has opened up for us. Saying we're sorry shows that we have come to the place of realisation that something is wrong. It indicates regret for what has happened, dissatisfaction with what we have done, and the intention of changing. There will be those who hope to change from lives dominated by addictions such as drugs or alcohol, but many more will simply need to reaffirm a commitment to growing ever closer to God.

It has been said that it's never too late to repent but it's never too soon either. Just as in our personal relationships we need to say 'I'm sorry', so it's also crucial in our faith and in our relationship with God. When we finally pluck up the courage to say the words, we're already experiencing the sense of relief and new potential. In that moment, the possibility of a new relationship is born. Although God loves us unconditionally, our prayer might be that God will love us anew as we try to move ever closer to him, responding in faith and action to his love. Our Christian faith calls us to repentance, not to be miserable in our sorrow but to adopt a new attitude. Being sorry isn't just words or even actions; it's an attitude of humility in which we see situations in a new way. So, even though 'sorry' may be the hardest word, it's well worth making the effort to say it on a regular basis.

Bible study passages

- Amos 4:1–13
- Mark 1:14–15
- Acts 2:37–42

Questions for discussion

- What is 'repentance'?
- Think of a time when you've had difficulty saying you're sorry. What happened?
- What has been your reaction when someone has said they're sorry to you?
- How easy or difficult do you find forgiveness?
- What examples of repentance can you think of from the Bible?

Further reading

Anthony Bash, *Just Forgiveness: Exploring the Bible, weighing the issues* (SPCK, 2011)
Irma Zaleski, *The Way of Repentance* (Continuum, 1999)

7

Becoming real: loved into life

Once upon a time there was a velveteen rabbit. He woke up one Christmas morning to find himself in a little boy's stocking with a pile of other toys. He was brand new and wondering what was going to become of him. When the little boy opened his presents, he was delighted with his new rabbit and played with him for hours, but soon the rabbit got put away in the toy cupboard and forgotten. He met lots of other toys in the cupboard, including the smart mechanical ones who thought they were 'real'. One of the best friends the rabbit made was the skin horse, who talked to him a lot and told him how important it was to become really 'real' and that this happened to you when your owner loved you. The rabbit listened to everything the skin horse had to say.

One day, the boy lost one of his other toys and the rabbit was chosen to take its place. The rabbit suddenly felt very much loved and wondered if he was at last becoming real. The boy took him out to play in the garden, where he met real rabbits. They teased him about not being real and how he hadn't got hind legs and couldn't run about. The velveteen rabbit longed to be real like the rabbits in the garden.

Suddenly, the boy became ill with scarlet fever and the

doctor ordered all his old cloth toys to be thrown out. The velveteen rabbit was gathered up with the rest and taken to the rubbish heap. Waiting in the pile of old toys, the rabbit felt very sad and rejected and began to cry. A real tear fell to the ground and, where it landed, a fairy with a flower appeared. The fairy lifted the rabbit up and carried him to the woods, where he met lots of real rabbits jumping around on their hind legs. The velveteen rabbit was so happy. Then, in a moment, the fairy turned him into a real rabbit. He ran around with the others and ended up making his home with them. Later, when the little boy recovered, he went out playing in the woods one day and saw some rabbits. He looked closely at them and could have sworn that one of them looked just like his old toy velveteen rabbit, but he never did find out what had happened.

The Velveteen Rabbit: or How Toys Become Real was written by the Anglo-American children's writer Margery Williams and published in 1922. It's a beautiful children's story with a number of very important themes for adults. In particular, it has several important Christian theological themes about the process of becoming real. It's particularly interesting how it reflects the idea of God as Trinity and his relations with the world.

First, in the cupboard the rabbit encounters the mechanical toys who think they're real. This reflects the increasing technology of the modern age and our sense that it provides or creates 'reality'. The story raises the question of what 'real' means, and the answer is that we become real when we're loved. The skin horse knows that being real means being loved. For the velveteen rabbit, the process of becoming real begins when he is taken out of the cupboard and starts to be loved by the boy. Next, there's the horror of being thrown away and destroyed. It's when the rabbit is lost and in despair that he begins to cry real tears. It's in rejection and crying that he starts to become real. Finally, when he becomes real, he leaps around with new life like the other rabbits: it's when he seems to have lost everything that he finally becomes real.

The parallels between the story of the velveteen rabbit and the Christian faith are worth pondering. Christian faith sees God coming in love to the lost. God comes to us in different ways but it's often when we're lost and rejected that we experience him. Indeed, he came in Jesus' life of humility, rejection, death and resurrection. Through the experience of loss, we can come to know the real value of our lives. More particularly, God's love for us in our loss helps us to become real in the sense that we know the real meaning of our lives as created by God: we are loved into fullness or 'reality'. Being real isn't about being mechanical or perfect. We learn about being real when we cry and when we're at the point of despair. That's the beginning, not the end of the journey. When our tears are real, God can take us and transform us into fully living beings. He loves us into reality.

There are also trinitarian parallels to the story of the velveteen rabbit. The experience of God as triune or threefold has its roots in the New Testament and was developed in the early centuries of Christianity. It focuses on God as Father, Son and Holy Spirit—a 'triune' God of three persons in one substance. The idea of God as triune focuses on God's love and relationship with the world through the life, death and resurrection of Jesus and through the Holy Spirit. Some of this can be felt in the story: God the Father loves us into reality; the pain of tears and rejection parallel Jesus' suffering and death; the new life or 'reality' at the end of the story is life in the Holy Spirit.

The story of the velveteen rabbit encourages us in faith, reminding us that God loves us in Christ, through all our pain and suffering, into the new life he gives us in the Holy Spirit. It's a wonderful and moving story with a powerful message for us today.

Bible study passages

- Deuteronomy 7:6–11
- 1 Corinthians 13:1–13
- 1 John 4:7–12

Questions for discussion

- Consider times when you've been shown love by someone and it has made a difference.
- Discuss a time when you needed love and couldn't find it.
- What does it mean to be 'loved into life'?
- How important are tears in your life?
- What other parallels can you find between the story of the velveteen rabbit and Christian faith?

Further reading

Margery Williams, *The Velveteen Rabbit* (Egmont Books, 2004)
W.H. Vanstone, *Love's Endeavour, Love's Expense: The response of being to the love of God* (DLT, 2007)

Jesus

8

Jesus Christ today: knowing, naming and following him

'Who is Jesus Christ for us today?'[11] This is the famous question asked by Dietrich Bonhoeffer from his cell in Tegel military prison, Germany, during the last 18 months of his life. Bonhoeffer had been arrested and imprisoned by the Nazis in April 1943. He was executed by hanging in Flossenberg concentration camp on 9 April 1945. During his months in prison, letters written to his fiancée and members of his family were smuggled out and taken to Eberhard Bethge, his friend and biographer. Bethge later edited the correspondence as *Letters and Papers from Prison*. In his hour of greatest darkness, Bonhoeffer struggled with the question of who Jesus Christ really is. Today, this prisoner of the Nazis is widely recognised as one of the 20th century's greatest Christian theologians.

Although Bonhoeffer's question originally came from his own desperate situation in prison, it is fundamental to Christians of all times. Who is Jesus Christ for us? What do we make of him? How do we understand him and what is his message for us now? Jesus himself asked his disciples the same question in the region of Caesarea Philippi: 'Who do people say that I am?' (Mark 8:27). The disciples' answers were varied, as the answers have been over the centuries since. In spite of the many answers given, though, the question remains central because it focuses the mind, heart and soul on the meaning of Christian faith. As Bonhoeffer knew, whatever answer we give, we cannot know Christ without following him and we cannot name him without knowing him.

What words would you use to capture the meaning of Jesus for you? In the Gospels he is given various names. At Caesarea Philippi the answers to Jesus' question all evoke part of the truth about him but none of them is adequate without the realisation that the disciples must follow him to the cross. In Mark 8:28, the answers are 'John the Baptist', 'Elijah' and 'one of the prophets'. The focus is on figures from the past, aligning Jesus with the prophets of Israel. Peter answers that Jesus is 'the Christ' (meaning 'anointed one'), even though he has little real concept of what this means. When Peter then challenges the idea that Jesus must suffer and die, Jesus says that Peter is on the side of Satan and focuses again on the necessity of his own coming suffering.

In the account of the same event in Matthew 16:13–20, Jesus asks, 'Who do people say that the Son of Man is?' thus providing the answer in the question. The term 'Son of Man' has a complex and mixed background but it's clear that it is associated in the Gospels with Jesus' suffering. The answers in Matthew include the names given in Mark, but 'Jeremiah' is added—which is significant, given Jeremiah's own humility and suffering (Jeremiah 20). In Luke's version (9:18–22), the answers are much the same as in the other two Gospels.

Interestingly, John's Gospel doesn't include the incident at all. Of course, in Mark, Matthew and Luke the answers all fall short of the truth, which can be perceived only through following Jesus and walking with him to the cross. In other words, anyone who wants to be a disciple of Jesus must have more than just the right words to name him; they must follow him and know his purpose intimately.

Other New Testament names for Jesus are familiar and still used today. For example, 'Lord' is often used of Jesus in the Gospels (Luke 24:34). It was clearly a title of respect as well as indicating Jesus' close relation to God. It's present in the very early Aramaic *maranatha* ('Our Lord, come!') in 1 Corinthians 16:22. It was also the word used to translate the divine name YHWH in the Greek version of the Old Testament.

Jesus is also 'Saviour' in the Gospels (John 4:42), which is actually what his name means, and 'Christ' or 'Messiah', the Greek and Hebrew words respectively for 'anointed one' (Mark 1:1; 8:29). He is 'Son of God' too (15:39). For Paul, Jesus is 'the power of God and the wisdom of God' (1 Corinthians 1:24) while in John's Gospel he is the Word of God (1:1). In a broader sense, Jesus is the crucified and risen one. Christians still use these expressions in worship and confession of faith today, but throughout the New Testament it's clear that names such as these can be fully appreciated only through knowing and following Jesus.

What might our own words and expressions for Jesus be? How would we name him in our own context of faith? Some of the New Testament words and expressions might not capture everything we want to say now. Christians today might think of Jesus Christ as 'superstar', as in the musical *Jesus Christ Superstar*. We might think of him as our 'friend' or 'fellow traveller'. He might be our 'leader', 'teacher' or 'guide'. Some might want to call him their 'companion' or 'soul friend'. All of these are attempts to capture who Jesus is for us—perhaps even to evoke further the depth of the mysterious grip he has on us—but none of them will be adequate or contain the deeper meaning of knowing him and following him in our lives.

Bonhoeffer's question 'Who is Jesus Christ for us today?' focuses our minds on who Jesus really is for us. We may be happy with biblical words and expressions or we may look for current equivalents, but in the end, whatever language we use of Jesus, whatever words we use to name him or to encapsulate his significance for us, we shan't really get anywhere if we don't truly know him and follow him. The naming includes the knowing, and following is connected with both of these. Bonhoeffer's own tragic experience taught him that the cost of discipleship is high. He was fully aware that the answer to his question involved following Christ all the way to the cross, and this is as true for us today as it was for him.

Bible study passages

- Jeremiah 20:1–18
- Mark 8:27–33
- Hebrews 1:1–14

Questions for discussion

- Why do you think Bonhoeffer's question is so important?
- Why did Jesus react the way he did to Peter's statement, 'You are the Christ'?
- Discuss the meanings of 'Son of God', 'Son of Man', 'Saviour', 'Lord' and 'Christ'. What do they say to you today?

- What does Paul mean when he calls Christ the 'wisdom of God'?
- What modern words or expressions would you use to describe the meaning of Jesus Christ for you?

Further reading

James Alison, *Knowing Jesus* (SPCK, 2012)
Dietrich Bonhoeffer, *Letters and Papers from Prison* (SCM, 2001)

9

Jesus the teacher: words and deeds

We can probably all remember particular teachers we had at school. Some stick in the mind as 'good teachers', but we probably remember others because we didn't like them, got on the wrong side of them or were hopeless at their subjects. The ones we remember best, perhaps, are those who somehow influenced us as people, leaving an impression on us beyond anything they taught us in class. You can probably remember teachers from your primary and secondary school days. There were probably similar individuals at university or in jobs you had, whose example and influence went beyond simply giving instructions. They were examples of how to live: they shaped our minds and possibly also our souls. They gave us more than information: they passed on something of who they were and what they stood for.

It's obvious from the Gospels that Jesus was a teacher. He is called 'rabbi' or 'teacher' more than once (for example, John 3:2; Luke 10:25). He teaches in parables as he brings the message of the kingdom of God and preaches to crowds of people in Galilee (Mark 4:1). It's easy enough to think of Jesus as a teacher in the simplest and generally accepted sense of the term. His parables are familiar to us from reading them in the Gospels and hearing them in church. The parables of the sower, the lamp, the seed growing secretly and the mustard seed (Mark 4:1–32), the good Samaritan (Luke 10:25–37), the lost sheep, lost coin and prodigal son (15:1–32), and the wise and foolish bridesmaids (Matthew 25:1–13) are all well-known, powerful stories. In John's Gospel, Jesus' teaching is rather different. Instead of parables, he teaches in extended blocks or 'discourses' (for example, John 14—17).

Yes, Jesus is clearly a teacher. Overall, it's easy to see that he stood in the tradition of the teachers of ancient Israel who used stories, parables and sayings to illustrate what they had to say. Prophets often used the 'comparison' (Hebrew *mashal*) to communicate their message, including the use of metaphor, allegory and analogy. All of this can be said of most teachers. We know that they use stories and that learners like them. A good story sticks in the mind and makes a point, and it should be remembered as easily as the message it illustrates. Jesus was certainly a good teacher in this sense.

The best teachers, though, do more: they embody their message in their lives. The prophets of ancient Israel not only preached the message of God's will to his people; they also performed symbolic actions that gave substance to their words. Hosea, for example, married an unfaithful woman (Hosea 1:2–9); Isaiah gave his children symbolic names (Isaiah 7:3; 8:1–4) and walked barefoot around Jerusalem (20:1–6); Jeremiah smashed a pot (Jeremiah 19:1–15), carried a yoke on his back (27:1–11) and bought a field (32:1–15); Ezekiel lay on his side for 390 days (Ezekiel 4:4–8) and shaved his head (5:1–4). For the prophets, there was more to a message than just the words. The message needed to be embodied and lived out in life. As teachers, the prophets were not just men of words; they were men of deeds as well.

Jesus was also, quite clearly, a man of deeds as well as of words. He not only gave a verbal message but also performed symbolic actions. In the early parts of Mark's Gospel, for example, he performs miracles: healing a man with a withered hand (3:1–6) and a woman with a haemorrhage (5:25–34), raising a young girl from the dead (5:21–24, 35–43) and restoring the sight of a blind man (8:22–26). In John's Gospel, in addition to the long discourses of teaching, Jesus performs 'signs' such as turning water into wine at a wedding in Cana of Galilee (2:1–11), and healing an official's son (4:46–54) and a sick man at Bethesda (5:1–9). The ultimate action that embodies his teaching is his death by crucifixion, a symbolic action far beyond that of the prophets of ancient Israel. In the cross and resurrection, the physical, visible side of Jesus' message is brought to its completion. All this illustrates that 'Jesus the teacher' is not just a man of words. He's a man of deeds as well. His teaching, healing, preaching, life, death and resurrection are all of a piece. To speak of 'Jesus the teacher' is to speak of all these aspects together.

It is commonplace today to separate the various parts of teaching. Education and learning get separated from medicine or healing. Preaching or religious nurturing get separated from both education and healing. In Jesus' day, people would have thought of all these as parts of a whole. Their understanding was much more holistic than ours: mind, body and soul went together as parts of a unity. So Jesus appears in the Gospels as one whose healing and preaching are part of his overall life as a teacher.

The best teachers we can remember from school or university, those who influenced us in work or in life, did so by giving us more than just information: they were examples of how to live. It's important to remember this in these days of increased educational opportunities and the 'information explosion'. There is more to Christian faith than information and facts, however important they might be. There is more to following Jesus than simply hearing the message or knowing the facts. There is more to following him than 'knowledge' in the narrow sense. Jesus calls us to more than information or knowledge. He calls us into a way of life, to follow him actively in his footsteps, setting an example and living out the message in our own lives. Imagine how we would grow in discipleship if we not only heard Jesus' message but also allowed him to influence the way we live.

Bible study passages

- 1 Kings 3:5–28
- Mark 1:21–22
- John 2:13–22

Questions for discussion

- What is the most important attribute in a teacher?
- Who was your favourite teacher and why?
- In what ways is Jesus a teacher?
- Consider some of Jesus' teachings. What do they say to you?
- 'Surely Jesus is more than a teacher.' What other words can be used to describe him?

Further reading

Morna D. Hooker, *The Signs of a Prophet: The prophetic actions of Jesus* (SCM, 1997)

Tom Wright, *Simply Jesus: Who he was, what he did, why it matters* (SPCK, 2011)

10

Jesus and healing: the new creation

I wonder if you've ever played any part in healing somebody. Have you ever had a role in helping somebody become whole? I don't mean 'Have you ever performed a miracle?' as much as 'Do you think in terms of healing and behave as if healing were possible?' Do you have an attitude of healing? For many people today, including some Christians, healing is something from the pre-scientific age. They don't expect it to happen now, but many others claim to know God's healing in their lives. The key is this: do we look for God's healing in the world? Do we have a positive attitude to healing? Do we do what we can to help it come about? Do we contribute to God's processes of healing?

A few years ago, I travelled through the Israeli-occupied West Bank in the Holy Land with a small group of women from Seattle. They were on a women's encounter course, meeting Palestinian women in Jerusalem, Ramallah and Nablus, as well as Nazareth inside Israel. In Nablus we visited St Philip's Hospital, where we crowded into a small ward to meet some of the patients. We were soon at the bedside of a Palestinian teenage boy who had fallen into an empty swimming pool, hit his head on the bottom and ended up in a coma. His parents and family were gathered around his bed in a state of shock and distress. Before I realised what was happening, a member of our group was moving her hands rapidly over the boy's body at a distance of a few inches.

I learnt later that the woman concerned was a practitioner of 'Healing Touch', a form of energy therapy founded and developed in the United States and now also known in Europe. Healing Touch is a bio-field, energy-field therapy, which works with energy and relationships in the pursuit of healing. Its aim is to restore balance in fields of energy and harmony in the body, and it is a holistic form of healing concerning itself with the whole person—physical, emotional, mental and spiritual. Linked to ancient wisdom and other faith traditions, it has been known to reduce pain, aid recovery after an operation, reduce depression and anxiety, and assist positively during chemotherapy and radiation therapy. It is complementary to traditional medicine and therapy methods.

When we left the hospital, the woman said she wished she'd had more time with the boy. His chances of survival were thought to be slim. We had prayed with his family for some time, and he is still alive today, though seriously ill. It struck me that far from being a 'new age' fad, 'Healing Touch' is a real attempt to engage with the divine life in creation. The incident brought home to me that we should be ready to assist in healing people wherever we find ourselves. As Christians, we are called to a healing ministry.

In the New Testament, Jesus is a healer and it's clear that his message of the kingdom of God involves healing. In the Gospels he heals at a number of different levels. In the early chapters of Mark's Gospel, for example, he heals people who are sick: a leper (1:40–45), Jairus' daughter and a woman with a haemorrhage (5:21–43). There are other dramatic healings later on, when Jesus uses spittle to help heal someone (a deaf man with a speech problem in 7:31–37) or connects healing to prayer (the epileptic boy in 9:14–29). On occasion, we're told, Jesus heals many people (3:7–11). He also performs exorcisms or casts out demons from those who are possessed, such as the man in the synagogue in Capernaum (1:21–28) and the Gerasene demoniac (5:1–20). In addition, some of Jesus' other miracles can be seen as healings. For example, in the stilling of the storm (4:35–41), Jesus heals creation itself, bringing it to a healthy equilibrium as he calms the sea.

All these stories and many others in the Gospels indicate that Jesus was a healer and that he invited his disciples into his processes of healing. More than once, Paul says that God establishes a 'new creation' (Galatians 6:15; Colossians 3:10; 2 Corinthians 5:17) in Christ, and this is surely also a sign that God's ultimate purposes have to do with healing the world.

In all these stories, physical touch and faith play a serious part in the process of healing. The incident in the hospital in Nablus not only introduced me to 'Healing Touch'. More importantly, it reminded me that, as Christians, we have a responsibility to join in with God's processes of healing whenever we can. We have a responsibility to maintain an attitude of healing and to look for and enable it. Of course we're aware that while some people are healed, others are not. We know that this can be one of the most challenging things for faith, especially if we are sick ourselves, but healing isn't magical, mechanical or available 'on tap'. God invites us to join with him in his healing processes, gradually building up the 'new creation' spoken of by Paul. Indeed, we can all be God's agents of healing on earth, as the prayer attributed to Teresa of Avila, the 16th-century Carmelite nun, says well:

Christ has no body now on earth but yours, no hands but yours, no feet but yours. Yours are the eyes through which Christ's compassion for the world is to look out; yours are the feet with which he is to go about doing good; and yours are the hands with which he is to bless us now.[12]

The prayer reminds us that Christians can participate in the work of Christ on earth. We are called to develop an attitude of healing, enabling it wherever and whenever we can, and we are called into God's ministry of healing, playing our part as best we can wherever we are in building up the 'new creation' in Christ.

Bible study passages

- Genesis 6:11–22
- Mark 4:35–41
- Galatians 6:14–16
- Revelation 21:1–4

Questions for discussion

- In what ways have you experienced healing in your life?
- What different sorts of healing are there?
- What are your impressions of 'Healing Touch'?
- What is the place of medicine in healing?
- In what ways does the whole creation need healing?

Further reading

Howard M. Ervin, *Healing: Sign of the kingdom* (Baker, 2002)
Eric Eve, *The Healer from Nazareth: Jesus' miracles in historical context* (SPCK, 2009)

11

Jesus and the poor: God in suffering

It's striking, isn't it, that God often comes to us in times of deprivation and loss, at times when we're most down and depressed, at our weakest and most vulnerable, and perhaps feeling least religious? It's true, of course, that we feel God's presence at times of beauty, joy, exaltation and happiness, but there's often a vivid, almost tangible dimension to God's presence in times of tragedy and grief.

In 1945, a Jewish doctor, painter and writer called Carlo Levi wrote his memoirs in the style of a novel called *Christ Stopped at Eboli*. The book tells of Levi's experiences in the early 1930s when, as a critic of Mussolini's fascist government in Italy, he had been exiled to the south of Italy, to two small villages in the area of Lucania. When Levi arrived, he found near desperation: extreme poverty, a variety of diseases and little medical care to speak of. Malaria was everywhere and the place was riddled with drunkenness, licentiousness and superstition. The inhabitants of the two villages said that Christianity, civilisation and morality had passed them by, that they had been left behind by the Italian government and by the society around them.

Most of all, they said, Christ himself had passed them by: he had stopped short of their villages at Eboli, further north. Eboli was the place where travellers always turned north and took a different road, so the villages of the south were never visited. Christ had done the same, they said.

Levi had a tough time getting initiated into village life but gradually offered his services as a doctor and became highly respected. When he was freed a year later, after the Italian war with Abyssinia, the inhabitants wanted him to stay and become mayor, but he left for Florence, where he wrote the book. He wanted to return but never did. The novel is a fascinating window on to life in that place in those days, a striking insight into poverty and desperation. The villagers thought Christ had passed them by, but had he? Was Christ not there with them after all? Perhaps he didn't stop at Eboli and turn north but was there all the time in the inhabitants of that place and in Carlo Levi himself as he ministered to the people.

It's important to remember that Jesus himself lived on the margins of society and showed a particular concern for the poor. The Sermon on the Mount (Matthew 5—7) and the Beatitudes (5:3–12) are especially significant here: it's the poor in spirit, those who mourn, the meek, those who are hungry for righteousness, and the persecuted who are 'blessed'. Jesus' life and teaching, as portrayed in the Gospels more widely, are also obviously focused on the lost and the deprived. His healings and miracles help those who are sick or possessed by demons (for example, Mark 5:1–20), many of his parables are about the lost and the marginalised (for example, Luke 15:1–32), and the kingdom of God is clearly characterised by concern for those who are in the greatest need.

In the Old Testament, where there are various views of

the poor, it's clear that God has a special concern for them. There are issues raised about economic poverty, social status and power. Certainly the poor should be protected (Leviticus 19:9–10). The prophets are particularly concerned about the polarisation of rich and poor, and the widespread oppression in society (for example, Amos 2:6–7; 4:1; 5:11; Isaiah 5:8; 10:1–2). Sometimes poverty is seen as the result of a person's own actions (Proverbs 6:10–11; 10:4), although in other places it is said that the poor should be defended (Job 29:12). In the Psalms, God is ready to help the poor: 'O Lord, who is like you? You deliver the weak from those too strong for them' (Psalm 35:10). All this forms the background to Jesus' concern for the poor.

In the 20th century the movement known as 'liberation theology' was founded and developed in South America and was involved with the poor communities in a number of different countries. Theologians such as Leonardo Boff, Gustavo Gutiérrez and Jon Louis Segundo wrote seminal works attempting to give voice to the oppressed communities of the area. Liberation theology begins with poverty, oppression, starvation and exploitation on the ground in particular communities and then seeks to address the structures of oppression and violence that allow the poverty to exist in the first place.

Liberation theology has developed in a number of different directions, including the 'Palestinian liberation theology' of Naim Ateek and others in the Holy Land. In England, Bishop David Sheppard's book *Bias to the Poor* took a similar line.[13] Feminist, womanist and gay theologies also seek to liberate the oppressed. Liberation theologians have not only started with the poor and tried to give them a voice; they have also actually found God revealed in the poor. Some have spoken of God's 'preferential option for the poor' and claimed that

God has a special interest in and concern for the poor and marginalised. This has sometimes been linked with the claim that God himself suffers with the poor and oppressed.

God often comes to us when we're weak and vulnerable, and he can often be found where there's loss and deprivation. In the Old Testament, he is concerned for the poor and the marginalised, and Jesus himself focused on the poor, the weak and the lost. In Carlo Levi's memoir, Christ surely didn't stop at Eboli. He continued to the villages where Levi himself ministered and was present in the poverty and suffering of the people. Liberation theologians recognise God's presence in the poor; Paul had his eye on this when he observed that God takes what is weak and makes it strong (1 Corinthians 1:25; 2 Corinthians 8:9; 12:10). God can often be found in places of weakness and suffering. Let us not miss him in the places where we might least expect to find him.

Bible study passages

- Psalm 35:1–10
- Luke 4:16–30
- 2 Corinthians 8:9

Questions for discussion

- In what ways do you think Christ was in Eboli?
- What situations of serious poverty have you known? Have they revealed God to you?
- What does the Bible say about the poor?
- What sense does it make to say that God has a special interest in the poor?

- What does it mean to say that God suffers with those who suffer?

Further reading

Gustavo Gutiérrez and Christopher Rowland, *A Theology of Liberation* (SCM, 2001)
Carlo Levi, *Christ Stopped at Eboli* (Penguin, 2000)

12

Jesus the good shepherd: door of the sheep

When I worked in the Holy Land with St George's College, Jerusalem, we often took groups to the Sinai desert to camp overnight under the stars on the way down to St Catherine's monastery. It was an amazing experience. Quite often I would be awoken at sunrise by the tinkling of small bells around the necks of sheep and goats being led by their shepherd through the cove where we were camping. Seeing them reminded me of Jesus the good shepherd—a rich and ancient image used of Jesus by Christians down the ages. Most of us are familiar with it from stained-glass windows, from statues showing Jesus carrying a lamb around his neck, and from Handel's *Messiah* or Bach's cantatas in which Old Testament passages about sheep are set to music.

It's important to remember, though, that it's not just Jesus the good shepherd we're dealing with in this image. It's also the idea of Christians as sheep, the ones who are protected and led by Jesus the good shepherd. He is the one who leads his sheep in the direction of food, water, sustenance and nurture. He is also the gateway or door into the fold.

Of course, it's not only Christians who have used the shepherd and sheep image. Most ancient societies applied the same image to their leaders and people. In ancient Assyria, Babylon and Egypt it was used for gods and leaders such as kings, warriors and princes. The coffin of Tutankhamun, for example, has a crook on it, showing that he was thought of as a shepherd. In ancient Greece the image was used for military leaders, and, indeed, the Greek god Hermes Chriopheros (ram-bearer) is depicted in statues with a ram around his neck. This is the image that the early Christians took and applied to Jesus the good shepherd. For nomadic and agricultural societies, the shepherd was and still is well known.

The ancient Israelites were certainly familiar with the shepherd and sheep image. God was seen as the shepherd who led the people of Israel to the promised land (see Psalm 78:52). In the story of Israel's return from exile, shepherd imagery is used (Jeremiah 23:1–4), and the most famous of all shepherd texts, Psalm 23, begins, 'The Lord is my shepherd, I shall not want.' God scatters the sheep (Psalm 44:11) and can be angry (74:1), and other shepherd-rulers have no understanding (Isaiah 56:11).

The famous King David of Israel is the classic shepherd figure. He was literally a shepherd from Bethlehem who rose to be the king of Israel (1 Samuel 16:1–23; 2 Samuel 5:1–5). Gradually, shepherd imagery was applied to leaders who would be raised up at the end of time (Jeremiah 3:15; 23:4). Worldly rulers were considered to be corrupt shepherds and, of course, God himself was the most important shepherd (Ezekiel 34). In Zechariah 9—13 (especially 11:4–14; 12:10; 13:7), God's shepherd will come from Davidic stock and will suffer for the sheep. This 'dying shepherd' tradition is also hinted at in Jeremiah's idea of the dying sheep who is a 'lamb led to the slaughter (11:19; compare Psalm 44:11; Isaiah 53:7). In both cases, one dies for the others. It's not difficult to see how these ideas influenced the Christian use of the shepherd image for Jesus.

In the New Testament, Jesus seeks out sheep that are without a shepherd (Mark 6:34). The parable of the lost sheep is well known (Matthew 18:12–14; Luke 15:3–7), and in Matthew 25:31–46 we find the parable of the sheep and the goats, about judgment at the end of time. Then, in 1 Peter 2:25 and 5:4 and Hebrews 13:20, the image is taken up in relation to Jesus and Christian leaders.

The most important text, however, is John 10, where we find the metaphor of the shepherd extended beyond the sheep to the sheepfold. Although Jesus is the good shepherd (v. 14), he is also the door or gate of the sheepfold (v. 7). The overall message is clear: Jesus himself is the way into the fold. There are those who try to break in by another way but they are thieves and robbers, and this is the thrust of the way the image is used in John's Gospel. Those who try to break in by another way, who try to steal their way in, cannot become part of the fold. This is most important: our faith in God cannot be stolen; the abundant life that God offers cannot just be taken. There is a particular way into the life that God offers.

The idea of Jesus as the door has caused some painful discussion recently, especially in interfaith contexts. If Jesus is the only way in, it is asked, can Jews, Muslims, Buddhists and Hindus, for example, not be part of God's fold? It's a crucial question, but the focus is surely on the type of life Jesus lived. There are certain requirements made of those who would enter the fold: there is a price tag on faith, a moral dimension to Christian believing. It's not just about 'believing in' Jesus but about committing oneself to his way of living. 1 Peter 2:20–25 brings out the important issue: Christians are required to be patient and long-suffering, not to revile when reviled, and not to insult when insulted. This is of the very essence of the Christian gospel.

The great image of Christ the good shepherd, so familiar to us from the Bible, Sunday school books, stained-glass windows and paintings, has much more wrapped up in it than the simple romantic image of a 'gentle Jesus, meek and mild'. It's an image including sheep, sheepfold and door. It points to the demands that are made of Christians and challenges us not only to follow the shepherd but also to enter the fold and live like him.

Bible study passages

- Psalm 23
- Matthew 18:12–14
- Luke 15:3–7
- John 10:1–18

Questions for discussion

- What are the strengths and weaknesses of the shepherd image for Jesus?
- What is it about Jesus that makes him 'the door' for Christians?
- Is the shepherd image still useful today, especially in urban societies? Give reasons.
- What images might replace the shepherd image?
- If Jesus is the door of the sheep, what about other religions?

Further reading

Brian D. McLaren, *Why Did Jesus, Moses, the Buddha and Mohammad Cross the Road? Christian identity in a multi-faith world* (Hodder and Stoughton, 2012)

Tom Wright, *John for Everyone: Part 1. Chapters 1—10* (SPCK, 2002)

13

Wisdom:
Christ himself

Late one evening, as I stood outside one of my churches in
Essex talking to a churchwarden, he suddenly said, 'Listen,
I think that's an owl.' We craned our necks and pricked our
ears into the night for a moment, hoping for another 'hoot',
but alas it didn't come. We parted company and I listened
all the way home in the hope of hearing or seeing the bird.
The incident reminded me that the owl can see in the dark
and stays awake all night, watching. It's vigilant and sees
everything. No wonder it came to symbolise wisdom. After all,
it's a wise old bird!

The owl was a symbol of wisdom in ancient times. It was
associated with the Roman goddess Minerva and Greek
Athena, the daughters of Jupiter and Zeus respectively. They
were goddesses of poetry, music, knowledge, medicine, com-
merce, weaving, crafts, magic and also of wisdom itself. The
owl became their symbol because of its wisdom. It also became
the symbol of philosophy because the word 'philosophy'
means the 'love of wisdom'. In the 19th century, the philosopher Hegel used the phrase 'owl of Minerva' to mean the

philosopher or the activity of philosophy. Over the years, wisdom has become associated with learning and politics, and many colleges and universities use the owl or one of the two goddesses, Minerva or Athena, as their symbol. The University of Lincoln, for example, uses the head of Athena as its logo, as does the seal of the State of California in the USA. In other places an owl is depicted. To this day, the all-knowing bird remains the symbol of wisdom.

Wisdom is important in Christian faith and life today, as it has always been. In the Old Testament a great deal is said about it. The so-called 'wisdom literature' (Proverbs, Job and Ecclesiastes) gathers together the traditions of the wise in ancient Israel. In Proverbs 8, wisdom is personified as a beautiful woman calling to those around her. She's depicted as being the first of God's creation, with him in the beginning before the mountains, hills and springs were created (vv. 22–31). Wisdom herself announces, 'Whoever finds me finds life' (v. 35) and Proverbs goes on to say, 'The fear of the Lord is the beginning of wisdom' (9:10). In later Jewish tradition, wisdom is depicted almost as a separate part of God's being, an aspect or element within God himself. It's certainly true that God's wisdom was central to ancient Israelite theology: it was bound up with the processes of creation and was part of God's way of relating to the world.

The early Christians took up the theme of wisdom and used it of Christ. For Paul, writing to the Christians in Corinth, Greece, in the early 50s of the first century, Christ is 'the power of God and the wisdom of God' (1 Corinthians 1:24). Paul is contrasting the wisdom of the world with the wisdom of God: 'God's foolishness,' he says, 'is wiser than human wisdom' (v. 25) and God has made Christ our wisdom. For Paul, Christ himself is God's wisdom because of his life, death and resurrection. Paul emphasises God's wisdom, not human wisdom. In later Christian theology the Greek word for wisdom, Sophia, became central.

An interesting development in our English Bibles can be seen in the well-known parable of the ten bridesmaids (Matthew 25:1–13). Ten young women, five wise and five foolish, await the arrival of the bridegroom. As they wait, the wise fill their lamps with oil while the foolish do nothing. Then, the foolish bridesmaids realise they need oil urgently and ask the wise for some of theirs. The wise will not give any away but send the foolish off to the shop to buy their own. While they're gone, the bridegroom arrives and the wise go into the wedding banquet with him. When the foolish get back with their oil, it's too late and they are excluded from the wedding banquet.

The wedding banquet is a well-known Jewish symbol for God's kingdom and reign. The wise are included, the foolish left out. However, in the original Greek, Matthew doesn't use the word *sophia* but another word, *phronimos*, meaning sensible, prudent or considerate. The bridesmaids are not portrayed as 'wise', just as 'sensible'. The point of the parable is 'be ready' or 'be prepared'. However, the translators of the King James Bible and of many other versions have used the English word 'wise', and the nuances are more profound. When the Lord is coming into our midst, it is wisdom we need, not just common sense.

People sometimes say that knowledge isn't enough in life. We need more: we need wisdom. This is certainly true in religion and faith. Knowledge of religious things, knowledge of the history of religion, doctrine or even its meaning isn't enough. Even knowledge of God in the sense of knowing things about God isn't enough. We need wisdom in order to appreciate what religion and faith are. A few years ago, the philosopher Nicholas Maxwell at University College London wrote a book called *From Knowledge to Wisdom: Revolution in the aims and methods of science*. He pointed out that even in science, knowledge alone isn't enough. Even scientists need wisdom when they investigate the universe.

So what is wisdom, and why is it so important? Wisdom looks for the inner meaning of things. It seeks insights into the deeper levels of reality and is marked by a humble and innocent approach to its subject matter. It is characterised by experience and not just rote learning. It has breadth and depth, and an openness to deeper learning, and seeks insight and appreciation. In matters of faith we must always seek insight through humility, hoping for a greater and deeper awareness of God in our lives. If Paul is right, in matters of Christian faith, Christ will be our main example. If we want to become wise owls, we should look at him.

Bible study passages

- Proverbs 8:22–36
- 1 Corinthians 1:20–25
- Colossians 1:15–20

Questions for discussion

- What do you understand by 'wisdom'?
- What was 'wisdom' in the Old Testament?
- How is human wisdom different from God's wisdom?
- In what ways is Christ our wisdom?
- In what ways can wisdom be seen in the world around us, in people or in the church?

Further reading

Katharine Dell, *Seeking a Life That Matters: Wisdom for today from the book of Proverbs* (DLT, 2002)
Nicholas Maxwell, *From Knowledge to Wisdom: A revolution for science and the humanities* (Pentire, 2007)

14

Justification by faith: computer studies

Sometime back in the late 1980s, I took an adventurous step and bought an Amstrad computer. Thinking of it now, it feels like a computer dinosaur. Actually, mine was only a word processor and I bought it partly, at least, under the sad illusion that it would somehow help me write a thesis. In fact, I did less work on the thesis in the initial stages because I was working out how to use the computer, but one thing I did learn fairly quickly was that, after typing in my text, I could press a particular key on the keyboard and 'justify' it. A fairly shabby-looking text can be smartened up to a high standard very quickly by 'justifying' it, and this means simply straightening the right hand side of the text. To justify the text is to make the right-hand side straight.

As a student of the Bible and theology, the language of 'justifying' struck me immediately, for doesn't Paul say that Christians are 'justified' by faith? Yes, he does, and there's an important connection here. The words that Paul and some Old Testament writers use mean 'to make straight'—the same as the typesetter's word for making the text straight. But of course there's much more to it than that. 'Making straight' is the literal meaning of the words and can be applied easily to a text, but Paul speaks of our relationship with God when he uses the language of justification, and of the role that the Jewish law and Jesus Christ play in it.

First of all, what do the words mean? In the Old Testament, the Hebrew word *tsedek* means 'to make straight' but it's used in a variety of senses that broaden its basic meaning. It's used, for example, in the song of Deborah when we hear of the 'triumphs of the Lord' (Judges 5:11). The word for 'triumph' is *tsedek*. From this it can be seen that the word is connected with the nature of God and his actions, the things he does for Israel. In 1 Samuel 12:7 the same word is behind God's 'saving deeds'. When the prophet Amos says, 'Let justice roll down like waters, and righteousness like an ever-flowing stream' (5:24), the word 'righteousness' is the Hebrew *tsedek*. It is also translated as 'justice' and as 'vindication'—for example, in Isaiah 51:4 and 62:2. It can be seen, then, that although the basic word means 'to make straight', it has other broader meanings, which involve God's very nature and actions, his righteousness and righteous acts, his vindicating power and his justice. Overall, it has to do with his 'right' and 'straight' dealings with the world.

By the time Paul picks up the word to speak of God's dealings with the world through Jesus Christ, it already has a long and complicated history. It has become a word used in the law courts of ancient Israel, still associated with justice but also now with acquittal and guilt. For Paul, Jesus Christ has overcome the Jewish law, which was the instrument used by God to bring about his good relations with the Jewish people. Jesus Christ, through his life, death and resurrection, has opened up new possibilities in the relations between God and humanity. For Paul, Christ is 'the end of the law' (Romans 10:4), its ultimate purpose and fulfilment. Paul uses the Greek version of the Hebrew *tsedek*—the word *dikaiosune*, which also means 'to make straight' and is connected to righteousness and justice. Paul explains that Christ is the path to God's righteousness (Romans 3:21–26), opening up the possibility of a new relationship with God and starting to make the way straight.

Paul's claim is that God has acted in Jesus in order to bring about the possibility of a new relationship. Paul's theology is rooted in his conviction that human beings have become separated from God by sin and that, by revealing himself in Jesus' life, death and resurrection, God has made a new relationship possible. The analogy of human relationships is very helpful here. A broken relationship, a falling out or a separation between friends or spouses needs someone to make a move, otherwise nothing will ever change.

When someone does make a move to apologise, the possibility of a renewed relationship opens up, and this is where the 'making straight' comes in: the relationship is 'straightened out' or mended and things are put right. 'Straightening out' is simply a metaphor for making a relationship what it was originally intended to be. If this is the case in human relationships, it is also the case between us and God. Our relationship is 'made straight' when we respond to God and when our relationship with God is good.

Most of us are aware of the expression 'justification by faith', but we may be less clear about where the words come from or what they mean. The claim that we're justified by our faith means that our relationship with God is 'made straight' in Christ. In him, the relationship is brought to what God originally hoped it would be. There have been many interpretations of exactly how this happens and the history of the theology of 'justification by faith' has been full of controversy. But the heart of Paul's theology is that God offers us new possibilities in Jesus and that, when we respond in faith and trust, our relationship with God is truly 'straightened out'. When we respond in faith, God's dealings with the world are also brought to their fullness.

Next time you justify the text on your computer, remember that you also can be 'justified' or 'straightened out', but your justification involves more than the click of a mouse. It comes through your faith in God, in Jesus Christ.

Bible study passages

- Genesis 22:1–19
- Romans 3:21–26
- Galatians 3:1–9

Questions for discussion

- What does the word 'justify' mean?
- What is the connection between 'justification' and 'justice'?
- According to Paul, what has God done to justify sinners?
- What part does faith play in justification?
- What is your response to God's work of justification?

Further reading

E.P. Sanders, *Paul: A very short introduction* (OUP, 2001)
Tom Wright, *What St Paul Really Said* (Lion, 1997)

15

Light:
standing in the river

One evening as I sit in my study, reading by a table lamp, a wasp hovers overhead for a moment, then makes for the light bulb. Finding the bulb hot, it moves to the inside of the shade and settles in the warm glow of the light. The event reminds me that human beings are also creatures of light and are drawn naturally to the light. Human life, animal life and plant life grow towards light. It's often striking to see a plant or tree grow around an obstacle towards a light source. Life needs light and has difficulty surviving without it; human beings enjoy light and seek it.

13 December is St Lucy's day. The name Lucy means 'light': the saint's life is associated with light and gave rise to different festivals of light in Europe. Lucy herself lived and died in the fourth century, martyred in the persecution under the Emperor Diocletian. Not much is known for certain about her life but it's said that her eyes were gouged out when she was martyred. In art, she is often portrayed with her two eyes on a dish in front of her. Eyes are vehicles of light that enable us to see: without them we're in darkness.

In Jerusalem, the well-known St John's Eye Hospital holds its service of light every year in St George's Anglican Cathedral. As part of the event, a pageant of 'Santa Lucia' is enacted. A young girl wearing a crown of real candles on her head processes up the aisle in a darkened church. Extremely moving, the scene portrays the fundamental significance of light as a natural symbol and a powerful religious image.

Light is a powerful symbol in the Bible. In the book of Genesis God creates light and darkness, and separates them: 'Then God said, "Let there be light"; and there was light. And God saw that the light was good' (Genesis 1:3–4). In the Psalms and Proverbs, light is a frequent symbol: walking with God is walking 'in the light of life' (Psalm 56:13), and God gives light to the eyes of the poor and the oppressor alike (Proverbs 29:13). The psalmist says, 'In your light we see light' (Psalm 36:9). Throughout the Old Testament, light is a symbol of God and the life he gives, a symbol of happiness, prosperity, learning and wisdom (for example, Psalm 97:11; 104:2; Proverbs 6:23; Isaiah 60:1–3).

In the New Testament, John is the key expositor of a 'theology of light'. In the Prologue to his Gospel we learn of the significance of the light, the Logos, that is coming into the world. John the Baptist is not the light; Jesus Christ himself is the true light (1:8). This becomes much clearer later when Jesus says, 'I am the light of the world. Whoever follows me will never walk in darkness but will have the light of life' (8:12).

After this, the first letter of John tells us that 'God is light and in him there is no darkness at all' (1 John 1:5). Light is also important in other parts of the New Testament. Jesus' own face shines with light at the transfiguration (Matthew 17:2). Christians are 'children of light' (Luke 16:8), their bodies when healthy are full of light (Matthew 6:22) and they are the 'light of the world' (5:14–16). For Paul, the light of

Christ exposes human beings and shows up their deeds. He writes to the Christians in Corinth that the Lord 'will bring to light the things now hidden in darkness and will disclose the purposes of the heart' (1 Corinthians 4:5). In Luke's Gospel, light signifies the salvation that is available to the Gentiles after the coming of Christ (Luke 2:32).

In the Bible, light is created by God but it's also a symbol for God's own life and the lives of those who come from him. To stand in the light is to stand in God's very life. This use of light imagery continues throughout the Christian mystical tradition in which the light of Christ is the goal of the spiritual life. To move towards God and to find union with him is to move ever closer towards the light.

Light imagery provides a powerful metaphor for our relationship with God, who pulls us towards himself. He is the life that we yearn for and in him we find the life we need. Light is the image, symbol or metaphor that evokes our relationship with God himself, his seeking of us and our movement toward him. The natural tendency of living creatures towards light, and the life and growth that light gives, are images of our growth towards the life of God.

Recently, at a service in London's Westminster Abbey, a slab in memory of the poet Ted Hughes was unveiled in Poets' Corner alongside many other famous poets. The words quoted on the slab come from Hughes' poem 'That morning' in his collection *River*. Hughes was on a trip to Alaska with his son. They were standing in a stream when a shoal of salmon passed by. The poet, struck by its beauty, writes:

So we found the end of our journey.
So we stood, alive in the river of light
Among the creatures of light, creatures of light.[14]

These words epitomise Hughes' incorporation into Poets' Corner among other 'creatures of light'.

More importantly, though, the words epitomise the spiritual journey we all make towards God. Like the wasp in my study, we're all drawn towards the light and we're drawn towards the divine light that pulls us ever closer. When we stand in the presence of God, therefore, we stand like Ted Hughes in a river of light.

Bible study passages

- Isaiah 60:1–5, 19–20
- John 8:12–20
- 1 Corinthians 4:1–5

Questions for discussion

- What examples can you think of where light is important?
- What different forms of light are there?
- How helpful is it to think of God as our light?
- Is God ever found in darkness? If so, when?
- What does Jesus mean when he says 'I am the light of the world' (John 8:12)?

Further reading

Ted Hughes, *River* (Faber and Faber, 2011)
Tom Wright, *John for Everyone: Part 1. Chapters 1—10* (SPCK, 2002)

16

Lineage:
the Christian family tree

Probably every family has a 'family history buff' somewhere in the wings, someone in the family who's interested in their ancestors and the family tree. In my family it was my uncle on my father's side, my father's brother. He had pursued family history for years and was always keen to tell us about it. He was always searching for that final missing link or unknown person to complete the picture. Periodically he presented us with the most up-to-date version of our family history, showing us what we knew and what we didn't know and where we all fitted in. A smart copy of our family tree, rolled up in a cardboard tube, would illustrate everything. My uncle's interest taught me a lot about the importance of our history as human beings, the need to know our identities, where we come from and how we fit into the wider picture of society.

Beyond a certain age many of us develop more curiosity about where we come from. Visitors to the UK from the United States, Australia, New Zealand and other countries with a connection to ours often appear in search of their ancestors' graves and wanting to dig through local records. Someone I knew who had been adopted as a child began searching for her birth mother because she felt a loss of identity. The TV programme *Who Do You Think You Are?* is all about helping people search through archives and records to discover their ancestors. The quest centres on questions of identity, meaning and the sense of a place in history. Without that sense, we feel lost and at sea. Our past is important to us and we like to know what it is.

Our Christian family tree is also important. After all, we didn't spring out of the blue and the Christian story doesn't start with Jesus. The beginning of Mark's Gospel takes us back behind Jesus to the prophet Isaiah, who is connected in the Gospels with John the Baptist: 'See, I am sending my messenger ahead of you, who will prepare your way; the voice of one crying out in the wilderness: "Prepare the way of the Lord, make his paths straight"' (Mark 1:2–3; compare Isaiah 40:3). The opening of Matthew's Gospel (1:1–17) takes the story through a lengthy family tree from Abraham to David and on to Jesus—a genealogy tracing Jesus' family tree back to his origins. Luke's version of the genealogy (3:23–38) traces Jesus back to Adam and the origins of the human race. John's Gospel takes us back to the beginning of creation, to a time before time: 'In the beginning was the Word' (John 1:1). The beginnings of the Gospels remind us that the significance of Jesus starts much further back than we often think.

In fact, it begins way back in the roots of ancient Judaism with the faith of the patriarchs and matriarchs, Abraham, Isaac and Jacob, Sarah, Rebecca and Leah. If you travel south from Jerusalem, past Bethlehem, you'll eventually come to the ancient town of Hebron in the West Bank. There, in a building erected by Herod the Great, you'll find the much older tombs of the patriarchs and matriarchs. The site is holy to Jews and Muslims and is shared by them today in synagogue and mosque.

The patriarchs and matriarchs are also our Christian ancestors. Their faith in the one God who revealed himself in the desert and inspired them to go out into the unknown is also our faith. It's an awareness of God that goes back millennia and has inspired generation upon generation to be courageous and bold. It's a faith, too, that inspired Jesus and his disciples, Paul and the Christian saints and martyrs down the ages. Paul himself knew of the importance of the faith of Abraham and refers to Abraham in his letters to the Romans (ch. 4) and the Galatians (3:6–18). In fact, for Paul, Abraham's faith was of the same pedigree as the faith of Christians.

The faith of Abraham, Isaac and Jacob, now coloured by Jesus, his death and resurrection, was also the faith that inspired one of the great Christian theologians and bishops of the fourth century, St Augustine. The life of Augustine is widely known and is told in his best-known work, the *Confessions*. He was no stranger to the lusts of the flesh and the pleasures of this world but his famous conversion led him to see that he stood in a long tradition of faith and that God's own presence had been known for centuries before him. Augustine was converted some time in his 30s and, once converted, he felt that he had wasted time in his youth. He wrote, 'I have learnt to love you late, Beauty at once so ancient and so new!'[15] He knew that the beauty of God's transforming presence in his life wasn't something that had sprung up anew with Jesus but had been there in creation from the beginning, from God himself. Augustine's understanding of the triune God—Father, Son and Holy Spirit—enabled him to appreciate the lineage and pedigree of his newfound faith.

Our family trees are important. They give us a sense of

identity and belonging. It's also important to remember that we stand in a long line of faith. Although it's important to look forward, it's also sobering to look back and remember our ancestors in faith all the way back to Abraham. We have a family tree that stretches back deep into the roots of Judaism and into the life of God himself. As Christians we are people with a family tree, a pedigree and a lineage. We have an identity rooted in the life of God and his ancient revelation to the human race. We are part of a 'footprint of faith' that stretches back thousands of years, a faith both ancient and yet always new.

Bible study passages

- Genesis 12:1–9
- Matthew 1:1–17
- Luke 3:23–38

Questions for discussion

- What do you know about your own family tree?
- Why is it important for people to know their family background?
- What gives you your main sense of identity?
- Why is Jesus' family tree important?
- In what ways are Christians connected to Abraham?

Further reading

Bruce Feiler, *Abraham: A journey to the heart of three faiths* (HarperCollins, 2002)
Tom Wright, *Matthew for Everyone: Part 1. Chapters 1—15* (SPCK, 2002)

Belief and practice

17

Baptism: a new beginning

In 1995 the African-American pop singer Tracy Chapman released an album called *New Beginning*. It wasn't her first. She was already well known for *Tracy Chapman* (1988) and *Crossroads* (1989). *New Beginning* immediately became very popular; it was another reflective and moving collection of songs that would help secure Chapman's name in the history of pop music. Born in Cleveland, Ohio, she rose from a poverty-stricken background, through busking in Harvard Square and an education at Tufts University in Massachusetts, to being a household musical name around the world.

It's Chapman's lyrics as much as her music that attract people. Focusing on poverty and human rights, the songs often have political or religious messages combined with a stirring acoustic guitar accompaniment. Among her best-known songs are 'Talkin' about a revolution' and 'Fast car'.

As her popularity has grown, Chapman has often sung at key events such as the 1988 Nelson Mandela Birthday Tribute concert, a number of Amnesty International events and the 'Make Poverty History Now!' tour. She always has something important to say and a very engaging way of saying it. The lyrics on *New Beginning* seem especially religious, speaking of love, desire and longing. The second song on the album is also called 'New beginning', and in it Chapman laments the many unhappy endings that life leaves, and encourages us to start again and make a new beginning.

The baptism of a human being marks a new beginning, a new moment in the person's life as well as for their family and church. As the person is immersed in or sprinkled with water, they commit to a new way of life and the whole community supports them. New beginnings are opportunities to start over and make a fresh effort. God himself likes new beginnings: he's always making them!

The Bible is full of new beginnings. From the time of creation to the life, death and resurrection of Jesus, there are many new beginnings, and they are often marked with water. In Genesis 1, when God creates the world (a very significant 'new beginning'), there's plenty of water about. At the time of the flood, when Noah makes the ark to save his family and the animals, there is also lots of water (Genesis 6—8). Water is featured when Israel passes through the Red Sea and into the desert (Exodus 14) and, when the Israelites finally cross into the promised land, they pass through the River Jordan (Joshua 3—4).

Water is also important in the life of Jesus. He himself is baptised in water by John the Baptist (Mark 1:9–11) and, in Cana of Galilee, he changes water into wine at a wedding (John 2:1–11). In Samaria he meets a woman at a well and offers her 'living water' (4:1–42) and, at the time of his death, water and blood come out of his pierced side (19:34).

Water is a powerful symbol in the Bible, and the reason is that it's essential to life. We can't live without water, and it's amazing to think just how much water there is on the planet. Seventy per cent of the earth's surface is covered with water. Sixty per cent of our bodies are water. Every time we take a bath or shower or have a swim, we are covering ourselves in water. When it rains, we get wet! Water is part of creation and is a blessing to us from God. In Hebrew the word *berakah* means 'blessing', and in modern Hebrew it's also the word for rain. In Israel 'We had an inch of *berakah* last week' means 'We had an inch of blessing or rain.' Water is indeed a blessing and in the biblical narratives it plays an important part in God's dealings with humanity. It's not only cleansing and refreshing; it marks boundaries and thresholds and new beginnings.

With water comes the Holy Spirit. In Genesis 1:2, at creation, the Spirit of God hovers over the water and plays a role in the formation of the world. In the Gospels, when Jesus is baptised, the Holy Spirit descends 'like a dove' upon him (Mark 1:10). So also, when we are baptised, the Holy Spirit comes to dwell with us and marks a new beginning. The coming of the Spirit is thus symbolised by water.

When we take water and pour it over those who are baptised, we mark a fresh start and a time for a new opportunity. God comes in his Spirit to the ones baptised and to the wider community that supports them. In the second century, the African theologian Tertullian (c.160–c.225) said that Christians are like fish because they are born in water. He knew that baptism is a rebirth. He knew the power of water and the symbolism of the coming of the Spirit, and he knew that all who are baptised into Christ's life are making a new beginning.

In the Holy Land, baptisms and renewals of baptismal vows are frequent in the River Jordan. Many Christians forget the date of their baptism but it's actually important to remember the occasion. At baptism we enter the Church, we join the Christian family and we begin along the road of discipleship with Christ. Baptism seals us into the life of Christ and the community of those who believe in him. It also commits us to certain responsibilities, such as rejecting evil.

Whenever you hear Tracy Chapman singing, listen to the words. If you happen to hear 'New beginning' remember your baptism. Remember your responsibilities as a Christian, the presence of the Holy Spirit in your life and the opportunities you have every day for making a new beginning. Remember that you are baptised into Christ, and be glad of new beginnings.

Bible study passages

- Exodus 14:21–31
- Matthew 3:13–17
- Romans 6:1–11
- Acts 19:1–7

Questions for discussion

- Consider times in your life when you've consciously made a 'new beginning'.
- When was your baptism and what significance does it have for you?
- What occasions are there in the Bible when water marks a new beginning?
- In what ways is water symbolic of new beginnings?
- Why do people need to be baptised?

Further reading

John Macquarrie, *A Guide to the Sacraments* (SCM, 1997)
Timothy Radcliffe, *Take the Plunge: Living baptism and confirmation* (Bloomsbury, 2012)

18

The body of Christ: respecting difference

On a recent visit to the concert hall at Snape Maltings in Suffolk, I became particularly aware of the need to respect differences. The concert hall at Snape is widely known as the music centre founded by the composer Benjamin Britten (1913–76). Along with his friend Peter Pears, Britten established the Aldeburgh Festival in 1948, and Snape gradually became its home. The hall was opened by Queen Elizabeth II in 1967 and has now become an international venue for concerts, with practice rooms and a main concert hall. Gustav Holst's daughter Imogen Holst contributed her father's library to Snape, which added to its resources as a centre for musical excellence.

The concert I heard included a Schubert nocturne for piano trio, a Mendelssohn string quartet, solo piano variations by Britten himself and a piano quintet by Frank Bridge. It was a glorious evening, watching the players make music together and produce amazing harmony from the many different parts. As I watched, I became increasingly aware of the different instruments: two violins, a viola, a cello and a piano. As the various musicians played their own parts, they listened attentively to each other. The excellent view I had from halfway down the hall enabled me see how they worked together to produce harmony.

The scene reminded me of the book written a few years ago by the composer, conductor and pianist Daniel Barenboim. Entitled *Everything is Connected: The power of music*, it illustrates how music is made up of different parts. In an orchestra or choir, for example, each instrument or voice has a different line to perform. Harmony is produced as the players come together through their differences. Each musician brings a different voice or melody which he or she contributes to the whole. In music, themes and melodies compete, but they can be heard together in harmony. Barenboim uses this insight to illustrate his view of human relations in society and between countries. Each society, community, country or person brings something different: we can't expect everyone to agree. In music, there are other voices to be heard and respected: it's as important to listen as it is to play. So also in society, we need to listen to each other, playing our different tunes but coming together as one. Differences have to be heard and respected if there is ever to be any harmony.

In 1999, with the Palestinian literary critic Edward Said, Barenboim founded the West-Eastern Divan Orchestra for Israeli Jews, Palestinians and others with this musical view of the world in mind. Both Jewish and an Israeli citizen, Barenboim wanted to open up new possibilities for exploring peace between Israelis and Palestinians. He saw that just as music is made up of contradictory and competing voices coming together in harmony, so society, with its conflicting and competing voices, could unite in harmony, given the right conditions. So his orchestra emerged from a vision of world peace based on music and respect of difference.

Paul's teaching about the body of Christ has much in

common with Barenboim's ideas about music. Paul's image of the Christian community as a human body is one of his most powerful. In Romans 12:4 he says, 'For as in one body we have many members, and not all the members have the same function, so we, who are many, are one body in Christ.' Paul's idea of the Church as the body of Christ is rooted in his metaphors of the family: God is father (1 Thessalonians 1:3), Jesus is son (Galatians 4:4), and Christians are God's children (Romans 8:16–17). They are all members of a family (Galatians 6:10) and part of God's household (Ephesians 2:19). It's within the context of a vision of family love for one another (1 Corinthians 13) that Paul develops his idea of the body.

In 1 Corinthians 12:12–31, Paul brings out his meaning in an amusing way. Bodies have different members and it wouldn't do if the body were just an eye or a foot: 'If the whole body were an eye,' asks Paul, 'where would the hearing be?' (v. 17). The different parts of the body are all necessary to the whole but they are not all the same parts. They must remain different so that they can make their distinctive contributions. They interact with one another to produce a whole effect: 'The eye cannot say to the hand, "I have no need of you", nor again the head to the feet, "I have no need of you"' (v. 21). Paul is clear that all are interdependent: seemingly conflicting parts all play a role in the whole. There are different gifts in the Church, including apostles, prophets and teachers (vv. 27–31), but they're all part of a whole.

Paul's message of the body resonates with Barenboim's musical analogy for society. The various parts are all necessary; the conflicting voices all need to be heard. The apparently contradictory parts should all be brought into the whole. In our church life, in parishes, dioceses, within the different communions, across the worldwide Church, and even between the many different faith communities, this message is crucial. We're not all called to agree. We're not all called to play the same tune. We're called, rather, to respect differences, to listen, to hear the other voice and to know that there can be harmony, not by having everyone playing or saying the same thing but by respecting differences and thereby producing harmony. And in the end it will be a harmony worth having!

Bible study passages

- Genesis 11:1–9
- 1 Corinthians 12:12–31
- Romans 12:3–8

Questions for discussion

- What experience have you had of people of different cultures or religious beliefs?
- What problems arise when people of different beliefs live together?
- Think of some examples of how conflict could turn to harmony if people accepted difference.
- What is Paul's teaching about the body of Christ?
- What are the limitations to Paul's idea of the body?

Further reading

Daniel Barenboim, *Everything is Connected: The power of music* (Phoenix, 2009)
Tom Wright, *Paul for Everyone: 1 Corinthians* (SPCK, 2003)

19

Humility:
the compassionate life

'Can't you have a bit of humility?' 'Can't you back off sometimes?' 'Do you always have to have the last word?' 'Who do you think you are?' How often have we said these words to someone, in a moment of anger, in an argument with a spouse, perhaps, or in some sort of row with a friend? How often have we had things like this said to us? Humility isn't a fashionable word in our societies today. We're mostly brought up to value competition and self-assertion, which put us above other people. In a culture that is particularly individualistic, we're encouraged to achieve, to take pride in our superiority over others, which tends to mean treading other people down, rather than being humble. Arguably, not only in society but in our education system too, humility is often considered a weakness, but Christianity has always valued humility, at least in theory.

I wonder what the word 'humility' conjures up in your mind. Perhaps you think of Mother Teresa or Martin Luther King—people who gave their lives to serving others. Perhaps you think of humility as an ideal that can never be reached, an impossible perfection. But we don't have to look far to find a range of examples of humility. If you go to Westminster Abbey in London and stand outside at the west end, you can look up and see the images of ten martyrs of the 20th century. The images, erected in 1977, include well-known names such as Martin Luther King, Dietrich Bonhoeffer, Archbishop Janani Luwum and Oscar Romero. One image among them, whose name may not be so familiar, is Maximilian Kolbe.

Kolbe was a Polish Franciscan priest who supported persecuted Jews in Poland during the rise of Nazism in the 1930s. In the early 1940s he was arrested for this activity and taken to Auschwitz. One day, a prisoner escaped and it was decided that the inmates should be punished. Ten men were chosen to be starved to death. One man in particular became hysterical and broke down, so Kolbe offered to take his place. The men were starved for weeks and died at different stages but Kolbe survived. He was eventually killed with an injection of carbolic acid.

The story of Maximilian Kolbe is one of the most heartrending examples of humility in the 20th century: a man gave his life for someone else in the most horrific circumstances. It's an amazing example of humility and service to others, and Kolbe was made a saint in the Roman Catholic Church in 1982. Of course, in addition to the great acts of humility recorded, there are hundreds of humble acts and humble people that will never be known or remembered.

The *Oxford English Dictionary* defines humility as 'the quality of being humble or having a lowly opinion of oneself'.[16] The word comes from the Latin *humilitas*, meaning 'earthy' or 'lowly'. Humility is important throughout the Old and New Testaments. In the book of Proverbs, for example, humility has precedence over honour: 'The fear of the Lord is instruction in wisdom, and humility goes before honour' (15:33; see 18:12). In the New Testament, humility is everywhere. In the words of the Magnificat, the mighty are brought low and the humble and meek are exalted (Luke 1:51–52). In Luke also, the parable of the wedding supper indicates that putting ourselves in humble positions is important (14:7–11). The one who goes into the wedding feast and sits at the top table gets moved down, whereas the one who sits at the bottom of the table is invited to the top. Jesus adds, 'All who exalt themselves will be humbled, and those who humble themselves will be exalted' (v. 11). In Matthew 18:4, Jesus encourages his disciples to become humble like a child in their search for the kingdom of heaven.

Paul draws attention to the humility of God in Christ, when he speaks of Christ humbling himself unto death: 'And being found in human form, he humbled himself and became obedient to the point of death—even death on a cross' (Philippians 2:7–8). It's because of this humility that God then exalts Jesus. Christ is our example, above all else, of the humble life, and his humility forms the basis of the resurrection. In later Christian theology and spirituality, humility was often seen as an important virtue, for example by Augustine in the fourth century.

The writings of Karen Armstrong have become very popular. She has written many books on different aspects of religion, and a recent one is called *Twelve Steps to a Compassionate Life*. Compassion is close to humility and Armstrong reminds us that steps can be taken to achieve it, steps that will help us along the way to becoming more aware of our environment, of other people, of our relationships with them and of the importance of compassion. We may think that we can never reach the level of humility represented in some of the great saints. Thank goodness we're not all in the position of Maximilian Kolbe or called to do what he did, but we can carry out small acts of kindness, compassion and humility. Humility begins with us personally, wherever we happen to be, in our everyday relationships with one another.

Of course, we can't expect to do it all at once: humility takes time. Like an athlete or musician, we need training. Living a life of humility and compassion brings us closer to God and reminds us of our dependence on him. It reminds us of God's own humility in coming to us in creation and in the life of Jesus, and it reminds us of our supreme model, Jesus himself, and the example of humility he gave us. Being humble takes focus, time and determination, and the training can last a lifetime, but it's worth the effort and enables us to grow closer to God himself.

Bible study passages

- Isaiah 50:4–9
- John 13:2–11
- Philippians 2:6–11

Questions for discussion

- Think of a compassionate person you have known. What were they like?
- What is the relation between compassion and humility?
- What is humility and how important is it in Christianity?
- Where have you seen humility recently?
- In what ways was Jesus humble and compassionate?

Further reading

Karen Armstrong, *Twelve Steps to a Compassionate Life* (Bodley Head, 2011)
Stephen Cherry, *Barefoot Disciple* (Continuum, 2011)

20

Loving your enemies: Israelis and Palestinians

It's well known that Christianity tells us to love our neighbours. The expression 'love thy neighbour' has a special place in the English language and there was once a British TV sitcom with exactly that title. In the Gospels, the commands to love God and your neighbour are very clear. Indeed, these two commandments are found in Judaism and form the backbone of the Torah (Deuteronomy 6:4; Leviticus 19:18). The dual command is then carried into Christianity. In Matthew's Gospel, love of God and neighbour are said to be the basis of everything in the law and the prophets (Matthew 22:34–40) and Paul gives a similar message in Romans 13:8–10. In John's Gospel love of neighbour is summed up in Jesus' command to 'love one another' (13:34), and he expects his disciples to serve one another and wash one another's feet (v. 14). However, in the Sermon on the Mount, Jesus takes the idea a step further: the disciples are to love even their enemies (Matthew 5:43–48).

Loving your enemy certainly has a sharper sting than loving your neighbour or friend. Of course, a neighbour might be an enemy—but this is the point: we are to love, whoever our neighbour is. Just as the good Samaritan was neighbour to the man who had been attacked by robbers (Luke 10:25–37), so we are to be neighbours to whoever comes before us. Jesus' command to love our enemies cuts to the root of the gospel message and demands more than we usually want to give. The command to love your enemy cannot be taken lightly. It's a serious daily challenge, especially to those who live in difficult political circumstances.

The conflict between the Palestinians and Israelis comes to my mind at the mention of loving our enemies, like a classic test case. The Western media usually present the conflict in black-and-white terms, but it's more serious than that, including many different shades of opinion and dozens of different political and religious views. Particularly important in terms of loving your enemy is the fact that there are those on all sides who seek peace with their so-called enemies. Israeli Jews and Palestinian Muslims and Christians can often be found working together for the cessation of the conflict, for a peaceful resolution and towards a just peace for everybody. Far from a situation in which all Israelis and all Palestinians simply hate each other, there are numerous examples of how people on all sides have taken significant steps to love their enemies. It's surprising how quickly prejudice and fear can be broken down and 'enemies' who are not really enemies can become friends.

A lot of individuals in the situation have tried to help an enemy. A Palestinian has given water to an Israeli soldier in the desert; Israeli Jews have given blood to dying Palestinians during an army invasion, and there are also a number of longer-term efforts, such as peace projects that try to draw the various sides together.

One example is Seeds of Peace. Started in 1993, it runs a summer camp every year in the USA, at which adult mentors take charge of teenagers from the various communities in Israel-Palestine. Gathering on neutral ground away from the conflict, they encounter their 'enemies' in a place that allows strangers to meet in peace and trust. A Palestinian teenager from the West Bank, for example, meets an Israeli Jew from inside Israel—or a conservative Jew from Jerusalem meets a Muslim from Hebron. Stories are told, experiences are shared and games are played. Through it all, a new possibility dawns on the various parties: 'We didn't know they could be our friends.' A couple of weeks pass and new relationships are made, friendships are struck up and trust is established. Then the young people go back home to the old context. Cynical onlookers question the long-term value of the peace camps, but others know that seeds can grow in such soil.

Another example of such a project is Kids4Peace, an organisation founded in the Anglican Diocese of Jerusalem in the mid 1990s. Starting at St George's Cathedral in Jerusalem, it has now grown to significant dimensions, with summer camps in the USA, Canada and Europe. The children are younger than those who take part in Seeds of Peace but the idea is basically the same. Open to Jews, Christians and Muslims, Israelis and Palestinians, the camp embraces the three faiths as well as the two peoples in the conflict. There's real encounter between 'others' who are perceived as enemies, between 'others' who are feared because of the context in which they've grown up, and between 'others' whose faith is different. In all the camps, barriers break down, bridges are built and new relationships are established. Again, there are problems because the situation back home in Israel-Palestine doesn't enable or encourage regular contact with 'the other'. Once the participants go home, prejudices are reinforced and the fear re-established, but in all this there has been significant growth. Not only have the teenagers themselves grown but parents from across the divides have become friends as a result of their children's participation in the camp.

Such projects, and many others like them in the troubled situations of the world, give a real sense of reaching out to the 'enemy' and perhaps realising they are not 'enemies' after all. They certainly set an example to us all, offering hope for the elimination of hatred. Jesus' command to love your enemies radicalises the command to love only your neighbour. As the Sermon on the Mount reminds us (Matthew 5:43–48) anyone can love those who love them. What is really gained by that? The greater love is to love the enemy, and Christians are challenged to respond to this command. The examples from Israel-Palestine give us hope that we too can reach out to strangers. Let's take these stories to heart as we try to find our way in our own situations of loving our enemies.

Bible study passages

- Leviticus 19:13–18, 33–34
- Matthew 5:43–48
- Romans 13:8–10

Questions for discussion

- Who are your 'enemies' and how do you define them?
- In what ways do you try to get to know your enemies?
- How do you define your friends?
- Why do you think Jesus said we should love our enemies?

- What is your view of the peace and reconciliation camps held for people in conflict?

Further reading

Joan Chittister and Saadi Shakur Chishti, *The Tent of Abraham: Stories of hope and peace for Jews, Christians and Muslims* (Beacon, 2007)

Mary C. Grey, *The Resurrection of Peace: A gospel journey to Easter and beyond* (SPCK, 2012)

21

Prayer: listening to God

Prayer is sometimes defined as 'talking to God' and, on the face of it, that sounds as if it might be a helpful definition. What we're doing when we're talking to God is praying. The *Oxford English Dictionary* defines prayer as 'a solemn and humble request to God... a supplication, petition, or thanksgiving, usually expressed in words'.[17] But the idea that prayer is 'talking to God' is actually seriously misleading or, at any rate, only part of the truth. Instead, I suggest that prayer should be thought of primarily as 'listening to God', 'being in God's presence' or 'attending to God'. When we think of prayer, the emphasis is too often on talking. Prayer is first of all coming into God's presence in silence and humility and 'listening'.

Also, prayer is often thought of, even by practising Christians, as 'asking for things'. Too often, we pray seriously only when we're in need of something, and then it turns into 'petitionary prayer', that is, making petitions or asking for things. But this is the least of what prayer really is. Prayer is much broader than 'talking to God' or 'asking for things'. It has many different dimensions. To be fair, the *Oxford English Dictionary* does add 'thanksgiving' to its definition of prayer and that begins to broaden out the definition a bit.

In recent years there's been something of a revival in meditation or contemplative prayer, and it's interesting to see how people of no particular faith or religious persuasion seek meditation in, say, the Buddhist or another Eastern tradition. Some people do know the need to be alone with God in silence, to achieve unity with creation and to try to listen to the heartbeat of the universe. All of this is important because prayer is primarily about coming into God's presence, learning to be still and clearing the mind of its many concerns and desires. It's only then that we can be still in God's presence and bring our hopes and aspirations to him.

Of course, there's no need to look outside Christianity to find the riches of meditation or contemplative prayer. We have centuries of spiritual writing, practice and tradition of our own. The monastic traditions, Eastern and Western, have much to teach us. In the fourth century, in the deserts of Egypt, people like St Antony and St Pachomius sought quietness and stillness away from the cities. In the centuries that followed, there were hundreds of men and women who went out into the Judean, Negev and Sinai deserts, either as individuals living in caves or as communities. The deserts were populated with monastic communities: St. Catherine's in the Sinai and Mar Saba near Bethlehem, where John of Damascus lived, come to mind as examples of communities that are still there today. In the desert, they found themselves drawn into a challenging encounter with God in silence and self-denial. Later, in the great Benedictine, Franciscan and Dominican traditions in the West, the same search for God in silence can be found. Much more recently, the Quakers have developed a strong tradition of silence in their worship.

These traditions help us to take a long look at the ways in

which we already pray. We go to church, to a service of one sort or another. It might be a Eucharist or a service such as Matins or Evensong. We might be lifted up to the presence of God by hymn-singing and music. Hopefully we'll be nurtured in faith through confession, scripture readings and a sermon. There might also be some silence drawing the congregation together before they go back into the world to live out the faith they have professed together at the service. Worship like this will include thanksgiving and praise as well as petition, but, even with all these different aspects, such worship can be far too 'wordy'. A great deal could be gained by having more silences in public worship. Very often, people are better able to find silence in quiet times in their own homes or in particular places of solitude. Going on a retreat can help in entering into the silence that we so lack during the rest of our lives.

It's important to cultivate times of silence at some stage during the day if we're ever to be with God and find him successfully through prayer. In prayer we come into his presence, letting go of our busyness and taking the time to stop and be still. We live in a world where there is a great deal of talking and noise, and not much silence or listening. Prayer is about being quiet, about clearing our minds and hearts and opening a space for us to hear what God has to say to us. In Psalm 46:10, God says, 'Be still, and know that I am God!' It's in our own stillness that we move into God's stillness and listen to him.

What must we do in order to pray? It's not just about talking. Only when we come to God in a spirit of silent listening and thanksgiving will we be able to focus on bringing our concerns to him. We will not then just be 'asking for things'; we will truly know our need of God's help. The great medieval theologian St Thomas Aquinas (c.1225–74) said that when we pray for things, we're not trying to inform God about those things but reminding ourselves that we need God's help in them.

Following the monks and nuns of the great monastic traditions, we should first seek silence, listening to God in the depths of our hearts. Having reached that stage, we might then be in a state of gratitude rather than want, and free to talk to God openly.

Bible study passages

- 1 Kings 17:8–24
- Luke 11:1–13
- Romans 8:26–27

Questions for discussion

- What is prayer?
- How many different sorts of prayer can you think of?
- Where and when do you pray?
- What is contemplation?
- What is your understanding of intercessory prayer?

Further reading

Laurence Freeman, *First Sight: The experience of faith* (Continuum, 2011)

Martin Laird, *Into the Silent Land: The practice of contemplation* (DLT, 2006)

22

Icons:
looking through a window

Icons can be a very powerful aid to prayer. They're mostly found in Greek, Russian and other Orthodox churches but in the last few decades they've started to appear in the UK in Anglican churches and cathedrals. For example, Winchester Cathedral has nine icons by the Russian iconographer Sergei Fyodorov in a chapel behind the high altar. They include Christ (in the centre), the Virgin Mary, John the Baptist and St Swithun. Many ordinary parish churches these days also have an icon somewhere as an aid to prayer.

Orthodox Christians pray with icons and can often be seen kissing them and making the sign of the cross in front of them. Orthodox churches have icons on a screen, or 'iconostasis', separating the main part of the church from the altar area where the Eucharist or Liturgy takes place. The icon or image isn't just a religious picture or even religious art. For Orthodox Christians, it's a place of revelation or incarnation, where God's presence is made known through material, the wood and paint of the icon. Icons are often called 'doors of perception' or 'windows into eternity'. They lead the one who prays through the 'image' (which is what 'icon' means in Greek) to the realm of the divine, the world of God himself.

Icons focus upon a variety of different themes. The main subjects are the nativity of Christ, the transfiguration, the crucifixion, the resurrection, Pentecost and the Holy Trinity. There are also icons of the Virgin Mary and of the saints. One of the most well-known icons is the one of the Holy Trinity by Andrei Rublev, a 14th-century Russian iconographer. Based on the three visitors to Abraham in Genesis 18, it depicts the Trinity—Father, Son and Holy Spirit. It also depicts the Eucharist, as the three men are sitting around a table. There are many different layers of meaning to icons and they are full of rich images and symbols. They draw worshippers into their own space and invite them through the painting into the life of the divine.

In the early church, as soon as icons became popular, there were voices raised against them as people remembered the second commandment, 'You shall not make for yourself an idol' (Exodus 20:4; Deuteronomy 5:8). The Jewish people had followed this 'prohibition of images' in worship. The Muslim faith was to follow this prohibition even more completely later on. The Christians eventually allowed images, and people who prayed with them experienced God being revealed to them in a special way. Those who opposed such practices thought that there was a real danger of idolatry, of worshipping the icon or the image instead of worshipping God, and they became known as 'iconoclasts' or 'image breakers'. Thousands of icons were smashed and burnt in the famous iconoclasm controversies in the eighth and ninth centuries, when some of the Byzantine emperors forbade their use.

A very famous theologian of the time, John of Damascus (c.675–c.749), defended the use of icons in worship. Those who used them had been accused of idolatry and worshipping 'matter', but John replied, 'I do not worship matter; I worship the Creator of matter who became matter for my sake.'[18] In other words, John was saying, God himself joined up with the material world when he became flesh in Jesus of Nazareth. The incarnation was the backbone of John's understanding of icons, and he claimed that those who broke images and wanted to ban the making of icons were actually denying the incarnation itself—denying that God could be made known in matter.

Finally, at a council in Nicea in AD787, it was decided by the church of the time that it was permissible to pray with icons, and there have been icons in Christian worship ever since. The use of statues in Catholic churches might be seen in a similar light, although Catholics don't hold statues in such high honour as the Orthodox hold icons. John of Damascus also made an important distinction between worship and honour. He said that worship was due to God alone, whereas people could honour an icon. Honour isn't worship, simply the highest form of respect.

There is certainly a danger in using icons in worship because our focus can stay on the surface, but if you use the icon properly and let your meditation and prayer pass through into the full depth of the icon, you will receive the full benefit. It isn't necessary to understand the detail of the symbols in an icon or to be informed about the history of the style. You simply need to be able to spend time in silence before the icon in order to let God speak to you through it. A verse of a well-known hymn by the 17th-century priest-poet George Herbert sums up the theology of icons. The hymn 'Teach me, my God and King, in all things thee to see' contains the following verse:

A man that looks on glass,
On it may stay his eye;
Or if he pleaseth, through it pass,
And then the heaven espy.[19]

GEORGE HERBERT (1593–1633)

In the Orthodox tradition, it's important that an icon be 'written' (or painted) in the context of prayer, usually in a monastic community. There is a special process by which icons are written, and there is a special manner in which they should be used. Properly understood, they can be an enormous aid to prayer, but plenty of time is needed. Look for an icon you like and find a quiet half hour to spend with it in prayer. You'll be amazed at its potential for calming and clearing the mind. Spend time looking at it and through it. Look beyond it, through the door or window of perception into the presence of God. In this way you can be drawn through the image ever more deeply into the life of God himself.

Bible study passages

- Genesis 1:26–27
- Exodus 20:4–5
- Colossians 1:15–20

Questions for discussion

- What experience do you have of praying with an icon?
- In what senses are icons 'windows' through which we can look for God?
- What is the connection between icons and incarnation?

- What are the main subjects of icons?
- What are the drawbacks of using icons?

Further reading

Jim Forest, *Praying with Icons* (Orbis, 2008)
Linette Martin, *Sacred Doorways: A beginner's guide to icons* (Paraclete Press, 2002)

23

Glorious food: the Eucharist

Whenever I think of food, I think of the well-known song from the musical *Oliver*: 'Food, glorious food'. It conjures up images of exotic banquets and unlimited eating. I also think of the saying 'You are what you eat'. It's true that whatever we put into our mouths forms and shapes us. Food has an immensely important place in our lives and in society generally. If we're lucky, there's plenty of it about; if not, life itself is threatened. Most of us like going out to eat an Indian or Italian meal, or perhaps staying in with a Chinese takeaway or cooking our own favourite dish. More or less everyone enjoys food—but food also lies at the centre of eating disorders of one sort or another. Obesity is developing into a serious problem in the UK. Anorexia is the opposite, starving yourself in pursuit of a particular body image. Eating disorders are common among those who want to control their bodies as well as those who eat to comfort themselves. And then there are those in the wider world who are starving through lack of food.

Not many people associate food with religion but there's a strong connection. Both food and fasting have played a significant role in religion and worship for centuries, and both men and women have, at times, almost starved themselves to death in search of God or some kind of enlightenment. Food has always been closely associated with God: from long before Christianity, people gathered to worship their god and have a meal in the name of that god. They celebrated a religious festival by eating a meal. They sacrificed an animal and ate it, believing they were participating in the life of the god they worshipped. Food and divinity were part and parcel of the same service of worship; both were basic to life. The god became present through an act of eating.

In ancient Judaism, people ate food as they worshipped. The Passover meal included unleavened bread (Exodus 12). Moses provided bread for the Israelites to eat in the wilderness: the 'manna' of the desert was the food of God (Exodus 16). Food appears frequently elsewhere in the Old Testament— for example, when the prophet Elisha feeds 100 men (2 Kings 4:42–44). In the prophets, food and the cessation of hunger are connected to the end-time messianic banquet (Isaiah 25:6–8), and, in Ezekiel's vision of the new temple in Jerusalem, there are all kinds of trees with fresh fruit (47:12). Images of food played a part in the way the ancient Israelites believed things would be in the fullness of time when creation was complete.

In the New Testament, the Gospels make a strong connection between Jesus and food, with Jesus' feeding of the 5000 being perhaps the best example. He feeds the crowd with bread and fish, and the baskets of leftovers are full to overflowing. The story occurs in all four Gospels (Matthew 14:15–21; Mark 6:35–44; Luke 9:10–17; John 6:5–14) and there's the feeding of the 4000 as well, in Matthew 15:32–38 and Mark 8:1–10. Jesus himself is depicted, especially by Luke, as a man who frequently attends meals (for example, in Luke 11:37–41). Most obviously, there's the Last Supper, the meal at which Jesus takes bread and wine and distributes them to his disciples (Matthew 26:26–29; Mark 14:22–25; Luke 22:14–23; compare John 13:1–20; 1 Corinthians 11:23–32). After the resurrection in Luke's Gospel, there's the famous story of the two disciples on the road to Emmaus (Luke 24:13–35), who encounter Jesus in the breaking of bread. Other images of grain and bread also appear in the Gospels (for example, Mark 2:23–28), and, in the discourse following John's version of the feeding of the 5000, Jesus himself is the food: 'I am the bread of life' (6:35). He himself has now become the bread that feeds his followers, the food from heaven. Finally, at the beginning of Acts (2:42, 46), the early Christians break bread together regularly.

Through the centuries, the idea of God becoming known in a meal permeated Christianity as the Eucharist became the central Christian act of worship for many believers. Of course, there are many different views of the Eucharist but the common element is the meal that brings everyone together. God comes to dwell with those who eat the food of the Eucharist.

Food brings people together. It brings strangers together and deepens the relationships of those who already know each other. Hospitality through food has always been the centre of community life. Gathering for a meal in even the most secular circumstances has more to it than simply the function of eating. It joins people in a sense beyond the food, bringing them into communion with each other. There's an intimacy in sharing food, a meeting of minds and hearts, and, as we have seen, the same is true in religion: eating and worshipping are two basic human activities, as they have been throughout history.

'Food, glorious food'; 'You are what you eat'. What's the message today? Just as, in the Gospel stories, Jesus feeds the multitude, so God feeds us with the abundance of his life in the Eucharist. In a special meal, a symbolic meal, God and his people are united through food. In the Eucharist, bread and wine become the focus of the presence of God among us.

Finally, if we are what we eat physically, we are also what we eat spiritually. The food of the Eucharist is spiritual food for us to feed on in God's presence. God feeds us with his abundant life in a meal in which we encounter each other and God together. At the Eucharist we feed on God's presence at God's meal, and so it is that, for Christians, the Eucharist is God's 'glorious food'.

Bible study passages

- Exodus 16:1–36
- Psalm 78:21–31
- John 6:35–59

Questions for discussion

- What is your attitude to food?
- What different theologies of the Eucharist are there?
- How often is the Eucharist celebrated in your church? Should it be more or less often?
- What is the connection between the Eucharist and food?
- How helpful is it to think of the Eucharist as 'God's food'?

Further reading

Angel F. Méndez-Montoya, *The Theology of Food: Eating and the Eucharist* (Wiley-Blackwell, 2012)
Ross Thompson, *The Sacraments* (SCM, 2006)

24

Fasting: training the soul

I believe there's a real value to fasting—abstaining from food and drink for a period of time with the intention of deepening your awareness of God. Of course, I can't pretend we live in a culture where fasting is widely valued or understood, even by Christians. Our consumer-driven society isn't particularly geared towards restraint of any sort. On the contrary, most people feel we should indulge our appetites to the utmost, in the name of fulfilment. After all, life is short so make the most of it: 'Let us eat and drink, for tomorrow we die' (Isaiah 22:13).

Most young people today aren't brought up in a spirit of self-denial, and even religion is often thought of in terms of fulfilment rather than denial. British society is gradually catching up with others in its level of obesity and, although some might consider fasting, it's usually for the sake of slimming, not religion. Although most people probably try to eat and drink sensibly and follow a healthy diet, the notion that there might be a religious value to self-denial isn't widely appreciated. For thousands of years, though, many of the world's religions have valued fasting of some sort, and not just in religious communities such as monasteries. There's an ancient wisdom attached to fasting: it sharpens your awareness of God and helps you appreciate the many blessings of life.

Fasting played a part in ancient Judaism, as can be seen from the Old Testament. The main fast was the one prescribed for the Day of Atonement (Leviticus 16:29), the most holy day of the Jewish year, but there were other occasions as well. Both Moses and Elijah fasted for 40 days at the mountain of God in Sinai (Exodus 34:28; 1 Kings 19:8), King David fasted in mourning at the deaths of Saul, Jonathan and Abner (2 Samuel 1:12; 3:35), and there were public fasts observed regularly by society in general (see, for example, Ezra 8:21–23). There were different sorts of fast but they usually focused on repentance and prayer.

We know that John the Baptist and his disciples fasted (Mark 2:18–20), although Jesus' attitude seems to have been a bit more ambiguous. In Mark 2, the point is made that while John the Baptist and his disciples fast, Jesus and his disciples do not. Jesus tells the people that while the bridegroom is present, they don't need to fast, but when the bridegroom is taken away then they must fast, indicating that after his death there will be a time for fasting (vv. 19–20). Having said that, Matthew's Gospel tells us that Jesus fasted for 40 days in the wilderness at the time of his temptations (4:2). Paul also fasted, at the time of his baptism in Damascus (Acts 9:9).

Down the centuries, Christians have always valued some sort of fasting. By the second century, Wednesdays and Fridays had become fast days and, by the time of the fourth-century Council of Nicea (AD325), the 40-day fast of Moses, Elijah and Jesus had become part of the church's calendar, as the period known as Lent. Of course, in the various desert monastic communities the monks fasted severely, eating only the bare essentials for survival: bread and water. Fasting was linked with prayer and penitence and developed into a major part of the religious life, which was characterised by self-control, self-restraint and self-denial. Later, in the Reformation period, there were objections to having specific times of fasting and the view emerged that it should be left up to the individual.

Fasting has played a part in many of the world's religions. In Islam, the month of Ramadan comes to mind. During this fasting month, Muslims go without food and water from sunrise to sunset. They are then allowed to eat and drink between sunset and sunrise. Every year this fasting is taken very seriously by practising Muslims and can be a great strain in a hot climate. It's not difficult, also, to find different traditions of fasting in the Buddhist and Hindu religions. Again, it's usually linked with meditation, prayer and an emphasis on humility.

What is the real issue where fasting is concerned? Certainly a disciplined approach to our bodily intake can be very beneficial. It isn't difficult to see, just in physical terms, how we can eat too much, how we can become lethargic or heavy through over-eating. An athlete, for example, needs a proper diet, and some sense of restraint is important for most people. For religious people, fasting is a spiritual discipline, which has been known to enable a heightened state of awareness and to increase the sense of God's presence. Overall, fasting can help us train our souls and grow spiritually. When it's linked with repentance and prayer, it focuses our bodies, minds and souls and makes us more aware of God's presence in our lives. It also makes us more grateful for the blessings we receive and gives us some solidarity with people who have little or no food.

Although it may seem strange in our culture today to consider fasting, it's clear that religious people down the ages have seen the value of self-denial and self-control with regard to eating and drinking. They've seen the value of restraint and discipline in 'matters of the flesh'. Old Testament prophets, John the Baptist, Jesus and Christians of different traditions have done the same, and our brothers and sisters in Islam and other faiths also set a good example through their commitment to fasting.

During Lent and, indeed, at any time, we can gain a great deal from fasting, within the bounds of good health. It's often said that it is better to take something on during Lent than to give things up, but there is value in having a Lenten discipline that will train us to concentrate on God and the things of God more than on our own physical appetites. Fasting is worth a try.

Bible study passages

- 2 Samuel 12:15–23
- Matthew 4:1–11
- Matthew 6:16–18

Questions for discussion

- Have you ever fasted and, if so, what were your impressions?
- What are the benefits of fasting?
- Why do monks and nuns fast?
- What is the connection between fasting and faith?
- What are the religious weaknesses of fasting?

Further reading

David Grumett and Rachel Muers, *Theology on the Menu: Asceticism, meat and Christian diet* (Routledge, 2010)
Dag Tessore, *Fasting* (New City, 2007)

25

The ten commandments: doing what you like

The fourth-century North African bishop St Augustine once wrote, 'Love and do what you will', which is often rendered 'Love God and do what you like.'[20] It sounds ideal—as if there were no moral requirements made of us as Christians. All we have to do is to love and we can do whatever we feel like doing. Actually, though, that's not what Augustine meant at all. The focus, for him, was that if we love, we will only like doing certain things—godly things. So doing what we like will automatically be the same as doing what God likes.

In the early 2000s, an American High Court judge, Roy Moore of Alabama, hit the international news by refusing to remove from his courthouse a 5000-pound granite block bearing an inscription of the ten commandments. Moore was a fundamentalist Christian who wanted to make the commandments as widely known as possible. He had installed the block in the courthouse when he took the job in Montgomery but was later told to remove it because it impinged US laws about religious freedom. He refused.

From the British angle, the incident looked somewhat odd,

as, here in the UK, with an established church in England and obligatory religious education in schools, it's hardly an offence to display the ten commandments in public. In the USA, though, with its separation of church and state and its constitution protecting religious freedom, it's against the law to display the moral code of the Jewish–Christian tradition when there are many other traditions that need to be respected as well. In the end, Moore was removed from office for refusing to take the image of the commandments out of the courthouse. The block was removed later, after he'd gone.

Moore wrote up the story in his book *So Help Me God: The ten commandments, judicial tyranny and the battle for religious freedom*. He now travels the US with the granite block, speaking about the importance of the commandments. One thing he has achieved through this is to bring the commandments into international focus and public debate.

The ten commandments occur in two books of the Old Testament: Exodus 20:1–17 and Deuteronomy 5:6–21. In Exodus, they're given through Moses on stone tablets in a dramatic event that takes place on Mount Sinai. In Deuteronomy 5, they're given to the Israelites directly by God (see v. 22). The story of Moses and the ten commandments was made popular by the 1956 film *The Ten Commandments* with Moses played by Charlton Heston. In Judaism, the commandments form an important part of the law or Torah of the Jewish people.

Like many other sections of the Bible, however, the ten commandments are often read out of context. In fact, they're usually read as if they are a set of universal moral principles that can be understood at face value and then judged for their usefulness or otherwise in general life, but it's important to read what comes before and after them in their context. The commandments are part and parcel of God's covenant established with ancient Israel at Mount Sinai, and they are specifically related to Israel's journey into the promised land. The ten commandments, therefore, must be seen as part of a process of establishing a people who are promised a land to live in and are then led to it by God.

It's often said that the covenant between God and ancient Israel is a bit like a marriage. A couple don't follow the marriage vows in order to establish their relationship. They establish their relationship first and make their vows later. In other words, the relationship comes prior to the code of practice. So also the ten commandments come into place after the relationship with God has been set up. They are not a prior way of establishing salvation; they're supposed to help the established relationship flourish. It's a matter of grace, not works. God invites his people into freedom through his relationship with them and then gives the commandments to help them along the way.

The ten commandments have also been important in Christianity. Numerous ancient churches in England have them written above the altar alongside the Lord's Prayer, the Creed and the Beatitudes. Together, these writings have formed the backbone of Christian living for centuries. In Matthew's Gospel, Jesus affirms that he has not come to abolish the law and the prophets but to fulfil them (5:17) and, although there is a different attitude to the Jewish law in Paul's teaching (for example, Romans 10:4), the ten commandments took their place at the centre of Christian faith from the beginning. They remind us that faith is about the whole of life, that it touches everything we do and that certain moral implications and requirements are part of our relationship with God.

Augustine's comment that we should 'love and do what we will' sums up the significance of the ten commandments.

'What we will' should be the things of God, and if the ten commandments were all we had, we could do a lot worse. Rather than restraining us or breaking our backs with rules, the commandments should be what we naturally 'will' as people of God. Through them, God invites us into a different perspective and a different sort of freedom. In the present day it's often thought that 'real freedom' is being able to do 'what you like', but for Augustine real freedom was to be found in keeping God's commandments and following in his steps. So the ten commandments invite us into freedom. They release us into a style of living that will establish freedom in our lives. Rather than constraining us, they can release us.

Properly understood, Augustine was right: we can 'love and do what we will'. There's a certain freedom in being Christian—but we need the help of the ten commandments. Roy Moore popularised the commandments in a controversial way. We should not forget their importance to us in daily life as we aspire to be the people of God.

Bible study passages

- Exodus 20:1–17
- Deuteronomy 5:1–22
- Matthew 5:3–12
- Matthew 6:7–15
- Luke 11:1–4

Questions for discussion

- How important is it to have rules in our lives?
- What are the strengths and weaknesses of having rules in our faith?

- What was the original context of the ten commandments?
- Do you think Christians should follow the ten commandments? Why or why not?
- Why might some say that the ten commandments are outdated?

Further reading

Joan Chittister, *The Ten Commandments: Laws of the heart* (Orbis, 2006)
Roy Moore, *So Help Me God: The ten commandments, judicial tyranny and the battle for religious freedom* (WorldNetDaily, 2005)

26

Growth and renewal: good soil

It's amazing how things grow, isn't it? The story is told of a young couple who bought a house with a large garden, including a lawn and an apple tree at the front. They decided they needed to 'clear the garden' and, in the process, chopped down the apple tree, dug out the root and poured in tree killer. They removed the lawn and put down concrete slabs, making space to park their car. The man went off to work every day and the wife looked after the kids. Eighteen months or so later, the shoot of an apple tree could be seen peeping up between the slabs of the car parking area. The sheer persistence of nature had won out; the strength of natural growth had prevailed. The apple tree was on its way back, albeit stunted by its surroundings.

Not so dramatic but still amazing is watching vegetables and plants growing in our gardens. The growth is visible and the speed and energy of nature are striking. More powerful than anything, perhaps, is seeing our own children and grandchildren (or those of friends and relations) growing up. Watching human beings grow is a truly sobering thing. How quickly they seem to spring up, how complex a process it is and how 'miraculous' it seems to be as we observe it! All these examples remind us in different ways of the power of nature to grow. Growth and renewal are part of the process of creation itself.

And yet, growth always needs the right soil or circumstances. There needs to be fertile soil and enough rain; there needs to be the right climate for things to flourish. Apple trees, vegetables, other plants, and human beings all need the right 'soil' in which to grow properly.

Jesus' well-known parable of the sower teaches us about growth. The sower goes out scattering seed, which falls on different types of ground. This parable can be found in three of the New Testament Gospels (Matthew 13:1–23; Mark 4:1–20; Luke 8:4–15), where it has an allegorical interpretation. In Mark 4, it begins, 'Listen! A sower went out to sow' (v. 3), but an important question arises: is the parable actually about the sower? In fact, the story and its interpretation don't focus on the sower or even on the seed, but on the soil or ground that the seed falls on to when it is sown.

It might be better to call this parable the 'parable of the good soil', for, although the good soil only appears at the end, that is surely the real focus. In the interpretation given in the Gospels, the seed is the word of the kingdom. The seed that falls on the path has fallen on those who don't understand and it is snatched away by evil. The seed that falls on rocky ground has fallen upon all whose faith has no root and who give way in difficulties. The seed that has fallen among thorns has fallen upon those choked by worldly concerns and wealth, and the seed that falls on good soil has fallen upon persons who understand and it is therefore fruitful.

The parable reminds us that growth needs good soil and

that we will flourish only when we have the right ground in which to grow. It's important to find the right soil to be who we are in responding to God's word, and responding is a process of growth in which we join with God for the purposes of renewal and new life. Seed growing in good soil isn't static or frozen, not a finished product or a perfected state. Similarly, the kingdom of God is a process, a movement, a developing reality in which we never reach the end of the road. We respond in ever-changing situations, called to move out beyond ourselves, to grow in ever new directions and to create fresh and fertile soil in our lives in which the word of God can grow.

The 17th-century priest-poet George Herbert wrote a beautiful poem called 'The flower', in which he draws attention to the connection between the natural world and our own lives. In writing about the power of nature to renew itself, he observes how this mirrors personal growth. The speaker in the poem marvels at the beauty of flowers in spring and then says that he has found new life in his own heart:

> *Who would have thought my shrivelled heart*
> *Could have recovered greenness? It was gone*
> *Quite underground; as flowers depart*
> *To see their mother-root, when they have blown;*
> *Where they together*
> *All the hard weather,*
> *Dead to the world, keep house unknown.*

The sheer strength of growth has renewed the speaker's sense of his own creative power. His 'shrivelled heart' has 'recovered greenness'. Later in the poem Herbert adds the following words:

These are thy wonders, Lord of love,
To make us see we are but flowers that glide:
Which when we once can find and prove,
Thou hast a garden for us, where to bide.[21]

It's amazing to see how things grow and spring up into new life. Throughout creation, there is persistent growth if the right conditions prevail, and even sometimes against the odds. Ideally, of course, there should be the right climate for nurture and nourishment.

It's the same in God's garden, where we are called to be rich soil, to be fertile and productive, to join with God in producing the fruit of the kingdom, and there will be different results at the time of harvest. Some will produce a hundredfold, some sixty, and some thirty. Not all are the same, but in the end all who have provided good soil for the kingdom to grow in are accepted by God.

Bible study passages

- Isaiah 41:17–20
- Mark 4:1–20, 26–32
- Acts 10:34–48

Questions for discussion

- Consider some examples of natural growth that have struck you.
- In what ways have you experienced growth in your life recently?
- What is the main point of the parable of the sower?
- What sort of growth does God want?

- What examples of growth have you seen in church communities?

Further reading

Craig L. Blomberg, *Preaching the Parables: From responsible interpretation to powerful proclamation* (Baker Academic, 2009)
Tom Wright, *Mark for Everyone* (SPCK, 2001)

27

Emmaus: the eyes of faith

During the last couple of decades or so, a series of fascinating coffee table books called *Magic Eye* have appeared in the shops. The books contain what, at first sight, look like fairly boring two-dimensional wallpaper patterns, but if you hold the pages close to your eyes and then move them slowly away, or if you concentrate hard on the pictures, looking 'into' them, you should soon be able to see a beautiful three-dimensional image that reveals, perhaps, a tiger in a field, a camel in the desert, a cactus in flower or some other stunning scene. It might be difficult to hold the picture in view and you might 'slip out' on to the surface. If so, you have to blink and start again.

Unlike the more recent popular 3D films, for which special glasses are worn, a certain amount of perseverance is required to see into Magic Eye pictures. Some people say they can't see them, however hard they try, and that's because the pictures aren't just 'given'. They require us to 'look' with special attention and perseverance beyond the surface.

There are parallels here with the 'eyes of faith'. Although there's nothing 'magical' about faith, it does require a particular way of looking at things in order to see into their depths. Participants need to look further than the surface to see what's hidden within. Believers may not see in this way all the time and might slip in and out of it, just as they do with Magic Eye pictures, and they will need to put some serious effort into the process of trying to see. There are differences between the two—but both Magic Eye and Christian faith have to do with perception or the way in which we look at things. Do we see only the surface or can we see more deeply into things?

The story of the risen Jesus appearing to two disciples on the road to Emmaus is one of the most beautiful stories in the Gospels. Found only in Luke 24:13–35, it's typical of his imaginative storytelling approach. A resurrection appearance story, it comes after the dramatic events of the crucifixion of Jesus in Jerusalem, and contains major themes of discipleship, the fulfilment of scripture, resurrection and the breaking of bread. It also contains a powerful and realistic theme of the ambiguity of perception that has much to teach us about faith today. In this story, the risen Christ is an ambiguous figure who is not easy to recognise or hang on to.

Luke begins by telling us that two of Jesus' disciples are making their way to a village called Emmaus, near Jerusalem, on the day of the resurrection. As they travel along, deep in conversation, Jesus draws near and speaks to them, but they don't know it is him. In fact, Luke says, 'Their eyes were kept from recognising him' (v. 16). The story is reminiscent of Jesus' appearance to Mary Magdalene in John 20:11–18, in that she also fails to recognise him at first. In Luke's story, Jesus asks the disciples what they are talking about and they marvel that he doesn't know what has been going on in Jerusalem in the past few days. Luke has the disciples recount much of the story of Jesus of Nazareth, 'a prophet mighty in deed and word before God' (v. 19). The themes of the fulfilment of prophecy from Moses onwards, of angels appearing at Jesus' tomb and of the importance of his suffering all lead up to the centre of the story, in which the disciples ask the stranger to have a meal with them.

Luke says that Jesus seems to be intending to travel further but they persuade him to come into the house with them. At the meal scene (painted so vividly by Caravaggio, 1571–1610), Jesus takes, blesses, breaks and distributes bread in a meal that echoes many others in the Gospel—not least the final meal that Jesus ate with his disciples the night before he died. The Emmaus meal is a post-resurrection meal and would have clearly signified the Eucharist for Luke's first readers. It's at the point in the story when the meal is taking place that the two disciples 'see into' the meaning of what is happening. Luke writes, 'Then their eyes were opened, and they recognised him' (v. 31). However, at that very moment, the risen Jesus vanishes from their sight. It's significant that, as Luke describes these events, he uses the language of perception: they don't recognise him; their eyes are kept from recognising him; they want to hold him without recognising him; then their 'eyes are opened' and they recognise him, but he disappears. The disciples finally make their way back to Jerusalem and tell the others what's happened.

What does this wonderful story tell us about faith? Not just that it's like a journey, not just that Jesus comes to us at surprising moments, and not just that he comes to us in the breaking of bread. It also tells us that the gift of Jesus' risen presence to us, the gift of God himself, is not a 'given', not something that we can just gaze upon. It's not something waiting to be found on the surface of things. Faith is not a magical thing but, like Magic Eye, it comes with perseverance, training and insight.

Like the disciples on the road to Emmaus, our seeing with

'eyes of faith' will come and go. It will be vivid and then disappear; our vision will often slip away from us. Our looking will involve patience and waiting, striving, effort and attention, and when we think we've grasped Christ, the vision will disappear from sight. He is not to be clung on to, constrained or controlled; nor will he be boxed in, contained or possessed. No, there is ambiguity in our perception of Christ as he moves ever onwards ahead of us, beckoning us to follow him.

Bible study passages

- Genesis 32:22–32
- Mark 8:22–26
- Luke 24:13–35
- John 20:11–18

Questions for discussion

- In what ways does faith involve seeing things in a different way?
- How useful is it to think of faith as 'insight'?
- Why are some people apparently 'blind' when it comes to faith?
- Why does Jesus sometimes seem elusive?
- In what direction do you think Jesus is calling you?

Further reading

A number of Magic Eye books are available, by different authors, published by Andrews McMeel.
Jim Forest, *Road to Emmaus: Pilgrimage as a way of life* (Orbis, 2007)

Afterword

For many people today, believers and unbelievers alike, Christianity is a set of beliefs that can be either accepted or rejected. They feel that it's up to individuals what choice they make, but this view misses the heart of what faith is all about. In reality, Christianity is a way of life lived in relation to a living God. Believers are invited into a way of living that only really makes sense from the inside. That way of life is an exciting challenge, pulling us forward into new awareness, new perceptions and new understandings. As Christians, we never stand still: we're always on a journey, always on the move.

Often, even practising Christians envisage a God who is distant and intervenes only occasionally (if at all!) in the world. Jesus may be seen as a wholly divine figure to be worshipped but one who remains distant from us as a human being. Christians who attend church regularly sometimes remain unaware of Jesus' importance as a teacher, preacher and healer. In the same vein, the coming of the Holy Spirit can often be seen as limited to particular moments in the church's year.

The reflections in this book attempt to cut through some of these popular misperceptions. They have arisen out of a conviction that God comes to us new every day, and that he comes to us in a process of encounter through creation itself, through Jesus and through our relationships with others. The sense that God 'wells up' through creation rather than 'comes down' from another zone is a liberating and refreshing change from the popular concept of God residing 'up there', distant from us and beyond our reach. The God envisaged here is one who is in the process of drawing the world to himself in an exciting ongoing project. He is a God who comes to us through a world charged with his presence and on fire with his Spirit.

The reflections here also come from a conviction that there is always more to learn from the historical Jesus and from the Jesus of the Gospels. Jesus was one who displayed humility and service, who washed his disciples' feet, taught, preached and healed, and whose life, death and resurrection transformed lives. It's through his life that we can glimpse God and make sense of the claims of his divinity. What we see in his life, death and resurrection reveals the glory of God to us. As Christians, we're invited into the story of Jesus, which takes us along the road to Emmaus where there are always new turnings and new pathways.

From this point of view, Christian faith and life can look rather different: repentance, baptism, humility and the Eucharist seem more directly relevant; prayer, eating, fasting and following the ten commandments take on new dimensions and seem less daunting; key theological ideas such as transfiguration, resurrection and new creation become three-dimensional.

Christianity is more a 'way of life' than a set of beliefs, more a pattern of living than a set of abstract principles. Of course, there are teachings to be believed but they only make sense within the context of living them out. Christian beliefs only really make sense from the inside out, so I hope this book helps you journey deeper into the knowledge and experience of God.

Notes

1   Gerard Manley Hopkins, *Poems and Prose* (ed. W.H. Gardner) (Penguin, 1985), p. 27.

2   G.K. Chesterton, *The Wild Night and Other Poems* (Read Books, 2012), p. 18.

3   Clifton Wolters (trans.), *The Cloud of Unknowing* (Penguin, 1961).

4   Jacobus de Voragine, *The Golden Legend* (trans. Christopher Stace) (Penguin, 1998).

5   Julian of Norwich, *Revelations of Divine Love* (trans. Clifton Wolters) (Penguin, 1998), chs. 57–61.

6   Teilhard de Chardin, *Hymn of the Universe* (Collins, 1965).

7   Teilhard de Chardin, *Le Milieu Divin* (Collins, 1960).

8   Philip Larkin (ed.), *The Oxford Book of Twentieth Century English Verse* (OUP, 2002), p. 101.

9   Anselm of Canterbury, Proslogion 1, *The Prayers and Meditations of St Anselm* (trans. Sister Benedicta Ward) (Penguin, 1973), p. 244.

10 *The New English Hymnal* (Canterbury Press, 1986), No. 339.

11 Bonhoeffer's exact words are 'What is bothering me incessantly is the question what Christianity really is, or indeed who Christ really is, for us today.' Dietrich Bonhoeffer, *Letters and Papers from Prison* (ed. Eberhard Bethge) (SCM Press, 2001), p. 91.

12 The source of this quotation is obscure and there are various versions. On Teresa herself, see Rowan Williams, *Teresa of Avila* (Bloomsbury, 1991).

13 David Sheppard, *Bias to the Poor* (Hodder and Stoughton, 1983).

14 Ted Hughes, *River* (Faber and Faber, 2011), p. 74.

15 Augustine of Hippo, *Confessions* (trans. R.S. Pine-Coffin) (Penguin, 2002), 10.27.

16 C.T. Onions (ed.) *The Shorter Oxford English Dictionary* (Clarendon Press, 1973), p. 996.

17 Onions, *The Shorter Oxford English Dictionary*, p. 1647.

18 St John of Damascus, *On the Divine Images*, (trans. David Anderson) (St Vladimir's Seminary Press, 2002), p. 23.

19 *The New English Hymnal*, No. 456.

20 Augustine of Hippo, 'Homily on the First Epistle of St John' Treatise Seven, *Selected Writings* (trans. Mary T. Clark) (Paulist Press, 1984), p. 305.

21 George Herbert, *The Complete English Poems* (ed. John Tobin) (Penguin, 2004), p. 156.

Index of Bible study passages

Genesis 1:1–13 23
Genesis 1:1–31 136
Genesis 1:26–27 230
Genesis 6:11–22 176
Genesis 11:1–9 212
Genesis 12:1–9 .... 35, 203
Genesis 16:1–16 101
Genesis 18:1–15 69
Genesis 22:1–19 195
Genesis 32:22–32 253
Exodus 3:1–15 18
Exodus 14:21–31 207
Exodus 16:1–36 .... 110, 235
Exodus 20:1–17 243
Exodus 20:3–6 69
Exodus 20:4–5 230
Exodus 24:1–18 115
Exodus 32:1–29 154
Exodus 33:7–23 115
Exodus 33:17–23 18
Leviticus 19:13–18 .... 45, 221
Leviticus 19:33–34 221
Deuteronomy 5:1–22 243
Deuteronomy 6:1–9 45
Deuteronomy 7:6–11 162
Deuteronomy 26:1–11 125
Judges 7:1–25 149
2 Samuel 12:15–23 239
2 Samuel 15:30—16:4 40

1 Kings 3:5–28 171
1 Kings 17:8–24 226
2 Kings 2:1–14 59
Job 1:13–22 145
Job 2:1–10 31
Psalm 19 141
Psalm 23 185
Psalm 35:1–10 180
Psalm 74:12–17 87
Psalm 78:21–31 235
Psalm 93 129
Psalm 100 125
Proverbs 8:22–36 190
Isaiah 6:1–13 129
Isaiah 7:10–17 92
Isaiah 40:1–8 73
Isaiah 40:12–23 110
Isaiah 41:17–20 248
Isaiah 50:4–9 216
Isaiah 52:13—53:12 97
Isaiah 60:1–5, 19–20 199
Isaiah 60:1–6 27
Isaiah 66:5–14 106
Jeremiah 1:4–10 141
Jeremiah 17:5–18 120
Jeremiah 20:1–18 166
Joel 2:1–2, 12–17 31
Joel 2:28–32 64
Amos 4:1–13 158
Zechariah 9:9–17 40
Matthew 1:1–17 203
Matthew 2:1–12 27

Matthew 3:13–17 207
Matthew 4:1–11 239
Matthew 4:1–11 31
Matthew 5:21–48 97
Matthew 5:3–12 243
Matthew 5:43–48 221
Matthew 6:16–18 239
Matthew 6:19–21 154
Matthew 6:7–15 243
Matthew 13:44–46 154
Matthew 14:22–33 78
Matthew 17:1–8 115
Matthew 18:12–14 185
Matthew 19:16–22 23
Matthew 21:1–11 40
Matthew 25:31–46 .... 27, 129
Matthew 27:45–54 50
Matthew 28:16–20 120
Mark 1:14–15 158
Mark 1:21–22 171
Mark 1:21–28 145
Mark 4:1–20, 26–32 248
Mark 4:35–41 176
Mark 5:1–20 87
Mark 5:25–34 149
Mark 6:14–29 73
Mark 7:24–30 145
Mark 8:22–26 253
Mark 8:27–33 166
Mark 9:2–8 115
Mark 13:24–37 18
Mark 15:33–39 50

Mark 16:1–8.. 54
Luke 1:26–38 101
Luke 1:46–55 92
Luke 2:41–52 106
Luke 3:23–38 203
Luke 4:16–30 180
Luke 6:20–38 97
Luke 9:28–36 115
Luke 10:25–37 27
Luke 11:1–4 243
Luke 11:1–13 226
Luke 15:3–7 185
Luke 17:11–19 125
Luke 22:24–27 45
Luke 23:44–49 50
Luke 24:13–35 253
Luke 24:50–53 59
John 1:1–18 23
John 1:19–28 73
John 2:1–11 92
John 2:13–22 171
John 6:35–41 235
John 6:35–51 110
John 8:12–20 199
John 10:1–18 185
John 13:2–11 216
John 13:2–20 45
John 16:7–15 64
John 16:20–22 106
John 18:1–11 35
John 18:15–27 35
John 19:28–30 50

John 20:11–18 .... 54, 253
John 20:19–29 149
John 21:15–19 78
Acts 1:9–11 59
Acts 2:1–13 64
Acts 2:37–42 158
Acts 3:1–10 78
Acts 9:1–9 82
Acts 10:34–48 248
Acts 19:1–7 207
Romans 3:21–26 195
Romans 4:16–25 120
Romans 6:1–11 207
Romans 8:26–27 226
Romans 12:3–8 212
Romans 13:8–10 221
1 Corinthians 1:20–25 190
1 Corinthians 4:1–5 199
1 Corinthians 12:12–31 212
1 Corinthians 13:1–13 162
1 Corinthians 15:35–50 54
2 Corinthians 8:9 180
2 Corinthians 11:21–29 82
Galatians 3:1–9 195
Galatians 6:14–16 176
Philippians 2:6–11 .... 141, 216
Philippians 3:4–11 82
Colossians 1:15–20 .... 69, 136, 190, 230
Hebrews 1:1–14 166
Hebrews 10:26–31 101
Hebrews 11:1–12 149
2 Peter 1:16–18 115

1 John 4:7–12 162
Revelation 12:7–12 87
Revelation 21:1–4 176
Revelation 21:1–27 136

Meet Jesus

A call to adventure

John Twisleton

To engage with Jesus expands the mind and heart. It challenges our view of the way the world is, where it is heading and what difference we could make to it. But in a world of competing philosophies, where does Jesus fit in? How far can we trust the Bible and the Church? What difference does Jesus make to our lives and communities? Is Jesus really the be all and end all?

Meet Jesus is a lively and straightforward exploration of these and other questions, with the aim of engaging our reason, inspiring our faith and worship, deepening our fellowship and service, and bringing new depth to our witness to the world. Each chapter ends with some practical points for action and the book concludes with a section of discussion material for groups.

ISBN 978 1 84101 895 9   £7.99

Available from your local Christian bookshop or direct from BRF: visit www.brfonline.org.uk

Paul as Pastor

Biblical insights for pastoral ministry

Patrick Whitworth

When we think of the apostle Paul, 'pastoral' is not usually the first word that springs to mind. He may seem too intellectual, too tempestuous, even too determinedly pioneering, to fit into the 'pastoral' category. This book demonstrates that, at heart, Paul was indeed too multi-faceted in both background and ministry to be defined by a single function. He was an apostle, prophet, evangelist and teacher—but he was also a pastor.

Patrick Whitworth makes the case that Paul's extraordinary teaching was a product of his pastoral care, which was itself a product of his pioneering and prophetic evangelism. He was an inspiration to pastors everywhere, to be studied and emulated, fathomed and then followed.

The book includes a study guide with a wealth of questions for group discussion linked to each chapter.

ISBN 978 0 85746 046 2   £7.99
Available from your local Christian bookshop or direct from BRF: please visit www.brfonline.org.uk.

Moments of Grace

Reflections on meeting with God

Joy MacCormick

From desolation to celebration, loneliness to love, *Moments of Grace* offers pithy, thought-provoking reflections on themes connecting God, faith and the journey of life. Questions for further pondering help the reader make links between head and heart, between what they believe, what they wrestle with believing and what they experience day by day.

Joy MacCormick, a New Zealand Anglican priest, has written this book to help people have a closer encounter with God in prayer, especially those who may struggle to find a place in conventional church worship.

ISBN 978 0 85746 224 4   £6.99
Available from your local Christian bookshop or direct from BRF: please visit www.brfonline.org.uk.

Whole Life, Whole Bible

50 readings on living in the light of Scripture

Antony Billington
with Margaret Killingray and Helen Parry

Where we spend most of our time—at home, at work, in the neighbourhood—matters to God and to his mission in and for the world. Far from restricting our faith to the 'personal' sphere, disengaged from everyday living, Scripture encourages us to take the Lord of life into the whole of life.

Whole Life, Whole Bible is written from the conviction that God's word illuminates every part of existence, enabling us to see differently and live differently—from Monday to Sunday, in public as well as in private. A walk through the unfolding story of the Bible in 50 readings and reflections shows how our lives are bound up with, and shaped by, God's plan to restore a broken universe.

ISBN 978 0 85746 017 2   £6.99

Available from your local Christian bookshop or direct from BRF: visit www.brfonline.org.uk.

Lord... Help My Unbelief

Considering the case against Christ

John Young

This is a completely revised and updated edition of a best-selling classic (previously published as *The Case Against Christ*) to help those who want to understand the strong reasons for holding the Christian faith in today's world. John Young offers a jargon-free and highly readable exploration of what Christians believe and why—and includes some good jokes along the way!

With help from prestigious experts including Professors Richard Bauckham, John Polkinghorne and David Wilkinson, the author tackles issues such as the relationship between Christian belief and science, faith and suffering, the reliability of the Bible, the uniqueness of Jesus, the evidence for his resurrection, and the extent to which we can 'prove' the existence of God.

ISBN 978 1 84101 875 1   £9.99
Available from your local Christian bookshop or direct from BRF:
please visit www.brfonline.org.uk.

The Psalms

A commentary for prayer and reflection

Henry Wansbrough OSB

This is a helpful companion for anybody wanting to venture deeper into the book of Psalms for personal reading and prayer. It also offers guidance for those preaching the Psalms and using them for group study and worship.

Revised and expanded from readings first published in BRF's *Guidelines* notes, the book provides accessible comment and reflection on every one of the 150 Psalms in scripture. Henry Wansbrough draws on his years of living and working in the Middle East to provide insight into the historical, literary and cultural background, as well as showing how these ancient texts can still guide and inspire us in our Christian walk today.

ISBN 978 1 84101 648 1   £8.99
Available from your local Christian bookshop or direct from BRF: please visit www.brfonline.org.uk.

Enjoyed
this book?

brf

Write a review—we'd love to hear what you think.
Email: reviews@brf.org.uk

Keep up to date—receive details of our new books as they happen.
Sign up for email news and select your interest groups at:
www.brfonline.org.uk/findoutmore/

Follow us on Twitter @brfonline

By post—to receive new title information by post (UK only), complete
the form below and post to: BRF Mailing Lists, 15 The Chambers, Vineyard,
Abingdon, Oxfordshire, OX14 3FE

Your Details
Name _____
Address_____
_____
Town/City _____ Post Code _____
Email _____

Your Interest Groups (*Please tick as appropriate)

- ❏ Advent/Lent
- ❏ Bible Reading & Study
- ❏ Children's Books
- ❏ Discipleship
- ❏ Leadership
- ❏ Messy Church
- ❏ Pastoral
- ❏ Prayer & Spirituality
- ❏ Resources for Children's Church
- ❏ Resources for Schools

Support your local bookshop
Ask about their new title information schemes.